“One can only voice a vigoro
Johns sees clearly that the numl
on our view of the Bible has lef
liberalism and reactionary fundamentalism, neither of which can allow the biblical text its proper work of wonder and deconstruction. Having identified these lamentable options of disenchantment, Johns applies her energy and courage to the work of re-enchantment of Scripture that defies both of these modernist options. Her rich Pentecostal legacy lets her see that it is the free, unfettered, unrestrained work of the Spirit that inhabits Scripture and that may also inhabit our reading of the text. Such a reading leads us into the holy mystery where the otherness of God may meet us and invite us to alternative living. Johns's work is at once breathtaking and breath-giving in its expansive hopefulness.”

—**Walter Brueggemann**, Columbia Theological Seminary

“We live in a world in which the taming and domestication of Scripture is prevalent. In response to this, Johns—one of the leading Pentecostal scholars today—asserts in *Re-enchanting the Text* that ‘we need a Bible that opens for us a world of real presence.’ This world of real presence is an ‘enchanted world’ in which ‘reason and imagination are joined together in creative harmony’ and in which we are ‘ravished with wonder by both the beauty and the terror’ of Scripture. In this powerful and compelling analysis, Johns offers a way to ‘re-enchant’ Scripture that refuses domestication; sees the text's power to disrupt, redescribe, and reorient; and embraces a pneumatic imagination. She extends to the reader an invitation to enter ‘sacred scriptural space,’ a space that is living, creating, and ultimately transforming. For those who want and yearn for more, this book is a must-read.”

—**Lisa Bowens**, Princeton Theological Seminary

“This book amounts to a bold Pentecostal intervention in current discussions about the theological interpretation of Scripture. With verve, rigor, and creativity, Johns demonstrates how the Spirit's ongoing presence in the Bible-reading community makes the text come alive as a means of ongoing grace. Her vision for a Pentecostal ontology of Scripture is not just for Pentecostals—it is a gift to the church catholic, born at Pentecost.”

—**James K. A. Smith**, Calvin University; author of *How (Not) to Be Secular*, *Thinking in Tongues*, and *You Are What You Love*

“This book holds a timely invitation to come on a particular journey, one that asks how it is that sacred Scripture has become something less than a text through which the Spirit manifests and speaks. That is but one part of the journey, however, because the book also provides us a way forward from this predicament. This work demonstrates a certain verve and facility with the relevant issues, and it is at once both accessible and seasoned. Educators and church leaders who find such a journey important for those they serve would do well to start with this volume."

—**Daniel Castelo**, Duke Divinity School

"I have been waiting on this book from Johns since reading *Pentecostal Formation*. Her argument there that the Holy Spirit shapes human discipleship in the way of the anointed messiah and living Christ is here extended to show that the same Spirit does so through re-enchanting the human imagination to be curious about the strange and dangerous world of the Bible. Feast on this volume and open yourself up to God's mystery being unveiled in our daily lives, even in a late modern world."

—**Amos Yong**, Fuller Theological Seminary

"Johns exposes the shallowness of current perceptions of Scripture in many Evangelical and Pentecostal contexts and then invites us to inhabit a new world—a liminal space where the Bible opens us to the beauty and mystery of the triune life of God. Johns's vision of and for Scripture in *Re-enchanting the Text* calls us into deeper, richer participation in God's revelation and presence. This vision is vital to engage the next generation, whose members long for true spirituality and value authenticity."

—**Rev. Jacqueline Grey**, Alphacrucis University College, Australia

"Under the rubric of re-enchantment, Johns sounds a clarion call for rediscovering something that has been lost in the worldview bequeathed to us by the Western Enlightenment in all the regions and ecclesial traditions where its sway has prevailed. The domains of contemporary Evangelical Christianity have not escaped its influence—even and especially in the precincts of its reputedly 'high' view of Scripture. In terms of Scripture's own most-favored rubric, what has been lost is both the idea and the experience of 'the holy.' Johns traces the lineage of this loss in modern thought and Western Christendom, particularly in its ways of viewing and handling the biblical text. And for the household of faith, argues Johns, this has increasingly meant the loss of our own postmodern children, who are longing to inhabit a re-enchanted world and a re-enchanted text that would underwrite it. In the light of Pentecost, rather than the Enlightenment, Johns points the way to a re-envisioning and a re-experiencing of the biblical text as *Holy* Scripture in the presence of the *Holy* Spirit. In so doing, Johns has opened through this wide-ranging work an urgent, timely, and evocative discussion."

—**Rickie Moore**, Lee University

Re-enchanting the Text

Re-enchanting the Text

DISCOVERING THE BIBLE AS SACRED, DANGEROUS, AND MYSTERIOUS

CHERYL BRIDGES JOHNS

Baker Academic
a division of Baker Publishing Group
Grand Rapids, Michigan

Published by Baker Academic
a division of Baker Publishing Group
Grand Rapids, Michigan
www.bakeracademic.com

Printed in the United States of America

Library of Congress Cataloging-in-Publication Data
Names: Johns, Cheryl Bridges, author.
Title: Re-enchanting the text : discovering the Bible as sacred, dangerous, and mysterious / Cheryl Bridges Johns.
Description: Grand Rapids, Michigan : Baker Academic, a division of Baker Publishing Group, [2023] | Includes bibliographical references and index.
Identifiers: LCCN 2022043514 | ISBN 9781540965134 (paperback) | ISBN 9781540965615 (casebound) | ISBN 9781493436675 (ebook) | ISBN 9781493436682 (pdf)
Subjects: LCSH: Bible. | Christian life.
Classification: LCC BS538 .J59 2023 | DDC 220.6—dc23/eng/20230110
LC record available at https://lccn.loc.gov/2022043514

Baker Publishing Group publications use paper produced from sustainable forestry practices and post-consumer waste whenever possible.

23 24 25 26 27 28 29 7 6 5 4 3 2 1

To my grandchildren
Camdyn
Charlie
Tegan
Harper
Carter

I have hope that you will find the Bible to be a wild and enchanting space and that, in doing so, you will come to love God deeply and serve him faithfully.

In memory of the saints who read the Bible
in the presence of God
and who taught me to do likewise.

Contents

Preface

The seeds for this book began to germinate in the late 1980s. A leading Evangelical seminary contacted my husband, Jackie, and me about interviewing for positions—he as dean of the chapel and I as an assistant professor. As we navigated three days of interviews, members of this academic community were gracious hosts, but we could tell that some had a nagging suspicion of our label as "Pentecostals." On the last day, I met with the entire faculty in a teaching auditorium. They placed me on the main floor with the faculty surrounding me. For over an hour, the questions ensued. Finally, one faculty member spoke the unspoken: "Wouldn't you agree that your tradition, with its emphasis on experience, has a low view of Scripture?" I knew this moment was coming, the moment when I would need to distance myself from my wild and sometimes crazy heritage and seize the opportunity to join the ranks of "enlightened Evangelicals." Many scholars in my tradition had done so, and now it was my turn. Had I not worked so hard to get here?

As I sat there, I began to ponder the question and to recall precious saints in my tradition who loved the Bible to the degree that they seemed to *inhabit* it. They feasted on the Scriptures, eating the Word, taking it into themselves so that they and the Word of God seemed to merge into one. These people not only read and studied the Bible, they also memorized it, prayed it, sang it, and embraced it. How could anyone say they had a "low view of Scripture"? Furthermore, how could I throw them under the bus?

Jackie and I had known that this moment was coming, and we had discussed possible answers. He encouraged me to "be myself" and to be bold enough to offer the challenge of exactly who in the room had a low view of Scripture. I did just that, saying, "If anyone here has a low view of Scripture, it may be that it is you and not I, for 'my people' believe that the same Spirit who was present and active in the writing of the Bible is present and alive in its reading." Silence. This gracious community chose to extend invitations for Jackie and me to join them. We decided against it, knowing that there would always be a cloud of suspicion over our brand of faith.

In the years since, a lot has happened in regard to how Evangelicals read and understand the Bible. We've had strident culture wars in which the Bible has become a weapon and not just God's Word. In response, younger Evangelicals are searching for a better way of being Christian and a better way of reading Scripture. Scholars are starting to explore the implication of the Bible becoming trapped in a world in which perception is reality, and everything is a matter of hermeneutics. The lost language of metaphysics and ontology is making its way back into discussions of the nature of the Bible. Descriptors such as "real presence" and "sacramental," which were unthinkable during the high point of modernity, are again becoming part of the conversation. These discussions are timely because people are hungering for the deep mysteries that lie beyond the closed, immanent frame of the modern world. They long for enchantment.

I'm glad to see the changes, and this book is my offering toward that discussion. Some may think that my vision of a "Pentecost ontology of Scripture" reflects a worldview of the fifteenth century more than of the twenty-first century. Others will see it as "magical thinking," noting that my understanding of real presence is more about subjective experience than about objective reality. I ask that readers approach this book with an open mind and glean from it those aspects that can enrich and deepen their relationship with sacred Scripture.

I'm grateful for the opportunities given to me to explore dimensions of enchantment found in the festival of Pentecost—in particular, the Jameson Jones Lectures in Preaching at Duke Divinity School (1997) and the Smyth Lectures at Columbia Theological Seminary (2008). The ideas in this book have shown up in numerous other venues, such as the Society for Pentecostal Studies and the Wesleyan Theological Society.

The beginning section of this book is drawn from two previously published works: "Transcripts of the Trinity: Reading the Bible in the Presence of God"[1] and "A Disenchanted Text: Where Evangelicals Went Wrong with the Bible."[2] I'm grateful to have received permission from these publishers to include this material here.

Through the years of writing this book, Jackie David Johns has been my encourager and dialogue partner. Our conversations are the highlight of my day. His insight and wisdom go way beyond my pay grade. My daughters, Alethea and Karisa, have graciously given space as well as inspiration. Their support sustained me during the times when I thought it would be impossible to finish. Robert Hosack, acquisitions editor at Baker, believed in this project. Moreover, he patiently waited while I put it aside to finish another writing project and then helped me take it up again. My graduate assistant, Marsha Robinson, has been a gift. She aptly applied to this manuscript the skills from her day job as editor of publications for the Church of God of Prophecy.

It is my hope that this book will serve as a means of encouragement and empowerment for the many people who long for Bible study to be more than a rational exercise. If you are one of those people, I pray that my words will entice you to enter into the enchanted wonderland of the Bible, a place where, by the Holy Spirit, words convey the real presence of God. When you enter this space, there's no turning back.

1. Cheryl Bridges Johns, "Transcripts of the Trinity: Reading the Bible in the Presence of God," *Ex Auditu* 30 (2014): 155–64, www.wipfandstockcom.

2. Cheryl Bridges Johns, "A Disenchanted Text: Where Evangelicals Went Wrong with the Bible," in *A New Evangelical Manifesto: A Kingdom Vision for the Common Good*, ed. David Gushee (St. Louis: Chalice, 2012).

1

The Strange Silence of the Bible

Rationalistic minds here and there have . . . tried to reduce the mystery.

—William James, *Some Problems of Philosophy*

We live in a world that cannot abide silence. Whether walking around with earbuds connected to smart phones or eating in restaurants where multiple TVs are playing, people seem intent on filling every silent space with sound. Yet there is a silence that no one seems to mind, one that James Smart identified as a "strange silence." As early as 1970, Smart wrote that "the voice of Scripture is falling silent in the preaching and teaching of the church and in the consciousness of Christian people, a silence that is perceptible even among those who are most insistent on their devotion to the Scriptures."[1]

In the first quarter of the twenty-first century, the silence of the Bible is deafening. In so-called Christian countries, the Bible is rarely quoted in public. Speech is no longer seasoned with reference to biblical texts. Parents do not quote Scripture to their children. Even

1. James Smart, *The Strange Silence of the Bible in the Church: A Study in Hermeneutics* (Philadelphia: Westminster, 1970), 15–16.

in the churches, there is this strange and eerie silence. Discipleship programs and preaching are flavored with Scripture, adding verses here and there to support the topic at hand. But few people are involved in direct study of the Bible. Evangelical churches have little tolerance for the public reading of Scripture passages that contain more than a few verses; preaching has been reduced to sound bites from the Bible.

Americans, in the words of Gary Burge, "are in danger of losing the imaginative and linguistic world of the Bible."[2] It is hard to disagree with George Gallup's assessment that the United States has become a "nation of biblical illiterates."[3] For the majority of Christians in the Western world, their lack of regard for Scripture cannot be blamed on religious persecution or the dearth of Bibles. The basic issue is disinterest. Christians of *all* stripes spend more time attending to social media, television, video games, and pleasure reading than they spend reading, listening to, and studying the Bible. If they do read the Bible, they approach it with what George Barna calls "the religious equivalent of sound-bite journalism."[4]

Certainly, we cannot blame the current scriptural illiteracy on a lack of modern translations. In fact, there are a myriad of translations and more and more forms of electronic delivery of the biblical text. Even in times of deep economic recession, marketing of the Bible proliferates. Timothy Beal notes that biblical consumerism continues without any indication of slowing down. He quotes "a marketing executive at a major evangelical publishing company" whose research shows that "the average Christian household owns nine Bibles and purchases at least one new Bible every year."[5]

2. Gary M. Burge, "The Greatest Story Never Read: Recovering Biblical Literacy in the Church," *Christianity Today*, August 9, 1999, 45.

3. George Gallup Jr. and Jim Castelli, "Americans and the Bible," *Bible Review* 6, no. 3 (1990): 37–38.

4. George Barna, "Barna Studies the Research, Offers a Year-in-Review Perspective," Barna Group, December 20, 2009, https://www.barna.com/research/barna-studies-the-research-offers-a-year-in-review-perspective/.

5. Timothy Beal, *The Rise and Fall of the Bible: The Unexpected History of an Accidental Book* (Boston: Houghton Mifflin Harcourt, 2011), 35–36.

"Looking back from the millennial year 2000, the Bible's primary use as a means of saving souls and serving as a silent junior partner in the American market enterprise has not changed much over the past century, though Americans are much less familiar with what is actually in it," writes Kenneth Briggs.[6] It is a strange and disconcerting irony that in the midst of a wealth of biblical information, we live in the Dark Age of biblical illiteracy.

Modernity and Its Disenchantments

As much as we lament the high rate of biblical illiteracy, it should come as no surprise that Christians do not read the Bible—specifically, they do not read the modern version of the Bible. By "modern version" I mean more than just a modern translation. I am referring to the Bible as it has been conceived during the period known as post-Enlightenment or modernity. The modern version of the Bible is a different sort of Scripture than in ages past. Its words do not haunt us, filling our days with images and stories. It does not satisfy our longing for mystery.

The modern version of the Bible does not trouble our nights with apocalyptic images. The modern version of the Bible is not memorized. The modern version of the Bible is not one that people turn to in crisis, quoting texts as they walk through dark valleys. The modern version of the Bible is a book that has been stripped of its power. It is a text that is neither alive nor mysterious. It is a disenchanted text.

The disenchantment of the Bible is a vexing problem. Multisystemic, it correlates with the Enlightenment project of disenchanting the world. The Enlightenment, roughly dating from the mid-seventeenth century to the latter part of the eighteenth, set in motion forces that eventually stripped the cosmos of the presence of the supernatural. N. T. Wright notes that "the Enlightenment (whose leading thinkers included Hume, Voltaire, Thomas Jefferson, and

6. Kenneth A. Briggs, *The Invisible Bestseller: Searching for the Bible in America* (Grand Rapids: Eerdmans, 2016), 5.

Kant) was, in fact, for the most part an explicitly anti-Christian movement."[7] While Wright may be stretching the point about the explicit anti-Christian agenda of the Enlightenment, it is true that this period in history created a new vision of the cosmos. This new vision, one that operated out of natural laws that could be discovered, understood, and harnessed for the betterment of life, gradually stripped the world of belief in being under the control of supernatural power.

Many good things have come about as the result of the Enlightenment view of the world. This view led to the rise of science and scientific discoveries that together have created a world wherein diseases have been drastically reduced. Modern inventions have created environments for ease and comfort. Modern communication has effectively networked the entire globe so that humans can communicate in ways our ancestors never could have imagined.

As a result of this new vision of the world, people gradually lost a sense of the sacredness of the natural order. Creation itself became an object to be acted upon, lorded over, and conquered. Perhaps the most tragic outcome of the Enlightenment is how the natural world was transformed into an objectified reservoir regarded as there to be used (and abused) by humanity.

Corresponding to this new vision of the world, the Enlightenment brought about a new understanding of humanity. Sometimes this turn is called the "Copernican Revolution." Nicolaus Copernicus (1473–1543) gave the world a radically different hermeneutical standpoint. Instead of the sun, moon, and stars revolving around the earth, Copernicus proposed that the earth moved around the sun. This decentering of the earth marked a turn in history, one that was twofold: a turn toward the world as the object and a turn toward humanity as the subject. These metaphysical moves set humanity on a trajectory that is now beyond anything our forebears could have imagined. It is the irony of history that the discovery that the earth was not the center of the universe helped set the stage to move humankind to the center.

7. N. T. Wright, *The Last Word: How to Read the Bible Today* (San Francisco: HarperCollins, 2013), 91.

Before Copernicus, human beings were seen as part of a large and mysterious canvas, one that was painted by supernatural forces beyond the control of humankind. Charles Taylor describes this world as having three features:

1. People lived in a natural world that "had its place in the cosmos," one that "testified to divine purpose and action." Natural events such as storms, floods, and times of exceptional fertility were seen as "acts of God."
2. God was "implicated in the very existence of society." In other words, the ethos of earthly kingdoms was grounded in a heavenly kingdom.
3. "People lived in an 'enchanted' world," one that was filled with divine presence. This presence could, at any time, impinge on their daily lives.[8]

A key dynamic of pre-Enlightenment metaphysics was the belief that visible things have a real relation to invisible things. The natural world was sacramental, meaning that the supernatural and the natural, much like a Möbius strip, were woven together and could not be separated. Furthermore, things had a reality all their own, separate from human perception. People could *know* this world, but it was difficult to imagine that people had the power to *define* the world.

Following the discoveries of Copernicus—and later, Francis Bacon—the world lost some of its mystery; it became a place that could be explored, studied, acted upon. Isaac Newton furthered this new vision with his ideas that the world operated out of "natural laws" that could be discovered and even harnessed for the betterment of humankind. Newtonian physics dominated the post-Enlightenment period and set the rules for engagement with the world. Scientists strove to discover and eventually control the "laws of nature."

8. Charles Taylor, *A Secular Age* (Cambridge, MA: Harvard University Press, 2007), 25.

Along with this new vision of the world came the notion of "objectivity." The universe, no longer enchanted, became the object instead of the subject. This metaphysical turn freed humans from seeing ourselves as part of a larger canvas. Now we could stand back from that canvas and analyze it. We could define its parameters. We could paint our own canvas! This turn to the human subject was intoxicating, granting humanity a status we who live today take for granted.

By the seventeenth century, the newly freed human subject needed a power to complement its status: namely, the power of the human mind. The discovery and translation of the writings of Aristotle in the late medieval period granted ontological status to the natural world. As a result, the Neoplatonic line of thinking that for centuries had dominated the Western world, one in which the material world was a reflection of the real world of idealized perfection, gave way to the material world having its own inherent properties. Furthermore, these properties could be known by the senses. This belief can be summed up in the dictum, "There is nothing in the intellect that was not previously in the senses."[9]

René Descartes (1596–1650) helped usher in a new era, one in which the senses were viewed as secondary to "the mind." His dictum, *Cogito, ergo sum*—"I think, therefore I am"—has been misunderstood to mean that Descartes abandoned the senses as a means of knowing the world, or that he believed the material world did not have its own metaphysical reality. Descartes's concern was to lift human reason to a status over that of superstitious belief or sensory perception. In doing so, he helped pave a way for humanity both to lift up the material world and to exalt the human mind as a means of knowing that world. As Wright aptly observes, "The Enlightenment insisted on 'reason' as the central capacity of human beings."[10]

9. Thomas Aquinas, *Questiones disputatae de veritate*, trans. Robert W. Mulligan (Chicago: Henry Regnery, 1952), 2.3.19, available online at https://isidore.co/aquinas/QDdeVer.htm.

10. Wright, *Last Word*, 91.

Following Descartes, philosophers such as David Hume and Immanuel Kant rejected the idea that the natural world had its own metaphysical properties. The location of meaning moved significantly from the external world to the inner world of the human knower. In this move, reality became a matter of perception.

The move to the rational subject brought about the rise of what Taylor calls "the secular age," an age "in which the eclipse of all goals beyond human flourishing becomes conceivable; or better, it falls within the range of an imaginable life for masses of people. This is the crucial link between secularity and a self-sufficing humanism."[11] Taylor observes that "the great invention of the West was that of an immanent order in Nature, whose working could be systemically understood and explained on its own terms, leaving open the question whether this whole order had a deeper significance, and whether, if it did, we should infer a transcendent creator beyond it. This notion . . . involved denying—or at least isolating and problematizing—any form of interpenetration between the things of Nature . . . and 'the supernatural.'"[12] In other words, things became separated: the natural from the supernatural, nature from grace, mind from matter, reason from emotion, humanity from the natural world.

In spite of the rise of secularization, Christianity throughout the eighteenth and nineteenth centuries retained much of its enchanted worldview: belief in the supernatural, the Bible as divinely inspired, the existence of heaven and hell, angels and demons, and a strong sense of God's work in the world. Among some of the educated, Deism, the belief that God created the world but was not directly involved in its day-to-day affairs, became a way to navigate the tensions between the Enlightenment worldview and religion.

There is much to praise in humankind's transformation into the rational subject. It empowered humanity to seek out solutions to the world's problems. It enabled people to explore the depths of nature, harnessing its laws and generating some of the world's greatest

11. Taylor, *Secular Age*, 19.
12. Taylor, *Secular Age*, 15–16.

inventions. It created a healthy sense of individual identity and freedom, thereby paving the way for the development of democracies and belief in human rights.

Such power is intoxicating. We humans began to believe that, with reason and through scientific discovery, all the world's woes would be solved without the assistance of some divine power. What little of the sacred or the supernatural survived was relegated to the private realm or reserved for the naive, the poor, or the superstitious.

Perhaps no one better summed up the spirit of the Enlightenment project than William Winwood Reade. Writing in 1872, Reade expressed his generation's intoxicating sense of power and the growing disdain for religion: "When we have ascertained, by means of science, the methods of Nature's operation, we shall be able to take her place to perform them for ourselves. . . . Men will master the forces of Nature; they will become themselves architects of systems, manufacturers of worlds. Man then will be perfect; he will then be a creator; he will be what the vulgar worship as a god."[13]

In the twenty-first century, Reade's words seem incredibly optimistic and naive. Through the lens of hindsight, we can see how this belief in the human power to be "manufacturers of worlds" led to the gas chambers of Auschwitz, Japan's industrial military complex, and the United States's use of the atomic bomb. After many wars, the notion that humans "will be perfect" leaves a bitter taste in our mouths. In light of global climate change and massive oil spills, it seems a strange irony that we aspired to "master the forces of Nature." We now know that the fateful turn to the subject has become a burden as well as a gift, a curse as well as a blessing.

The Burden of Disenchantment

The sociologist Max Weber was one of the first to recognize and name this burden. Weber saw the connection between the rise of rational-

13. William Winwood Reade, *The Martyrdom of Man* (New York: Asa K. Butts, 1872), 514.

ization, the industrial world, and the ever-increasing disenchantment of the world. He understood that creation of the secular state had called humanity out of the "enchanted garden," filled with mystery and wonder, into a more bureaucratic, secularized place, where there was little room for such things.[14]

In particular, Weber noted the connection between Protestantism's attempt to prove its intrinsic rationality and the rise of a nonreligious secular state.[15] The modern secular world had little room for naive and superstitious faith. After all, superstitious faith had left Europe bathed in the blood of religious wars. There was a hunger for a safer, more scientific worldview. Disenchantment was a small price to pay for prosperity and peace. It was a burden that was necessary for true science to emerge.

Speaking to a group of students at Munich University in 1917, Weber made the following observation: "The fate of our times is characterized by rationalization, and above all, by the 'disenchantment of the world.'"[16] If students want to be scientists, noted Weber, then they must learn to bear the burden of disenchantment. They must abandon the old superstitious beliefs of religion. True scientists are to be astute, logical, and disinterested in religion. They should learn to trust only in scientific reasoning and take their place as makers of history without the supernaturalism of days past.

In his lectures, Weber acknowledged such fate would be too much for some. He told students that if they were not willing to bear the burden of disenchantment, they could go quietly away from the university to the place where "the arms of the old churches were willing to take them."[17] During the ensuing years, many eager Christian students faced the terrible choice between Christianity and science.

14. Max Weber, *The Sociology of Religion* (1922; repr. Boston: Beacon, 1993), 270.

15. Max Weber, *The Protestant Ethic and the Spirit of Capitalism*, trans. Stephen Kalberg (New York: Oxford University Press, 2010).

16. Max Weber, "Science as a Vocation," in *Essays in Sociology* (Oxford: Oxford University Press, 1949), 155.

17. Weber, "Science as a Vocation," 155.

Architects of the Soviet Union believed they had freed people from religious superstition and its corresponding oppression. In Russia and its conquered territories, it wasn't just the scientists who were asked to bear the burden of disenchantment: everyone was called on to leave behind superstition. Religion was defined, in the words of Karl Marx, as an "opium of the people."[18] During the mid-twentieth century, China joined its Russian counterparts in attempting to create a secular state. China replaced the sacral hegemony of rulership in the imperial age with an aggressive form of secular communist ideology.

In both the Soviet Union and China, the process of secularization was ruthless. Christians and other religious groups were systematically arrested, sent to labor camps for reeducation (a tactic still employed by China), and marginalized from society.[19] The irony of such tyrannical policies of secularization is that they created far more death and destruction than did the "superstitious" religions they were attempting to eradicate.

During this time, what may be called "high modernity," it wasn't just students of science or people in communist countries who felt the pressure to leave behind a supernatural, "magical" Christianity. European Protestants, in particular, began to feel the pressing call to be more "scientific" or risk being left behind in the Dark Ages. As Weber aptly notes, the spirit of Protestantism, with its emphasis on the individual and a strong work ethic, helped fuel the spirit of progress that created the modern world.[20] The chickens had come home to roost. The Enlightenment was biting the heel of one of its strongest proponents.

By the turn of the twentieth century, Protestant churches were feeling the sting of criticism that they were out of touch with the

18. See Karl Marx, "A Contribution to the Critique of Hegel's Philosophy of Right Introduction," in Karl Marx and Friedrich Engels, *On Religion* (Moscow: Progress Publishers, 1972), 38.

19. See Christopher Marsh, *Religion and the State in Russia and China: Suppression, Survival, and Revival* (New York: Continuum, 2011).

20. Weber, *The Protestant Ethic and the Spirit of Capitalism*, 60, 70.

modern world. Darwinism, along with scientism and rationalism, challenged their enchanted worldview, one composed of a literal creation and of miracles, heaven, and hell. In the universities, theology was dethroned as the queen of the sciences; many doubted that theology was any sort of science at all. In major universities, religion departments were sidelined, their budgets cut, and their faculty looked on with suspicion by those who believed themselves to be more enlightened. Science became the model for all disciplines that would claim to be academic. It soon became clear that Christian theology and biblical studies had to become more scientific or be left behind.

As the twentieth century emerged, theologians and biblical scholars eagerly rose to the challenge of gaining admittance to the scientific academy. What is often missed is that this great effort to be scientific led to the rise within Protestantism of both fundamentalism and liberalism. In their basic forms, fundamentalism and liberalism were disenchanted, modern forms of religion. The scientific era offered liberals and conservatives alike the intoxicating power to reduce truth to its "factual essence." Both forms of Protestantism understood their quest as finding and supporting the "facts" of their faith. In order to support their faith, scholars turned to the Bible to find "proof" and "evidence" of their belief in the validity of the Scriptures. In this quest, the Bible became a critical player in modernity's obsession with its own power.

For liberals, a search for a "factual" understanding of the world meant a turn toward the "higher criticism" of the German universities. The German model emphasized a "neutral scrupulous objectivity" and a "commitment to science in organic (naturalistic) evolutionary terms."[21] The Bible, within this context, came to be understood as a collection of historical human documents. Through the course of history, these documents underwent revisions from the religious communities associated with the texts.

21. Mark Noll, *Between Faith and Criticism: Evangelicals, Scholarship, and the Bible in America*, 2nd ed. (Grand Rapids: Baker, 1991), 32.

In order to be placed within the field of scientific study, Scripture was removed from any sense of it being a vehicle of supernatural revelation. It became a compilation of documents that contained historical records. Just as archaeologists attempted to mine the evolutionary journey of the earth, biblical scholars attempted to mine the evolutionary journey of the biblical text. During this period the Bible became trapped in history. Its robust reading of the world and its vivid eschatology were consumed within the eschatology of the Enlightenment, which emphasized a reading of history as human progress. N. T. Wright calls this reading "we know better now."[22]

Along with the German model of biblical scientific study, "experience" became another lens through which liberals could authenticate Christianity. Here the Enlightenment turn to the human as rational subject came full circle. Human experience and human perception determined reality. That perception did not need any authority outside of itself. It constructed the world. The autonomy of the human rational subject would later bear fruit in postmodernism's rejection of objective truth.

Conservatives of this era rejected the "new science" of the German model. The new science, with its "speculative hypotheses" and its rejection of supernatural revelation, was not a true science, they argued. They proposed that Darwinian evolution was unscientific because it was based on mere hypothesis.[23] Looking for a better scientific method, conservatives entrenched themselves in the earlier Baconian model of science. Bacon postulated that nature itself revealed inherent truth. Known as "Common Sense Realism," such thinkers argued that the world could be known directly and could be studied through careful observation.

Thomas Reid, the person most closely associated with Common Sense Realism, argued that God implanted within the minds of people

22. Wright, *Last Word*, 96.

23. George Marsden, "Everyone One's Own Interpreter? The Bible, Science, and Authority in Mid-Nineteenth-Century America," in *The Bible in America: Essays in Cultural History*, ed. Nathan O. Hatch and Mark A. Noll (New York: Oxford University Press, 1982), 79–100.

"self-evident first principles."[24] These principles, such as the existence of God, are the starting point from which other knowledge would be built. The Baconian method of objective and empirical analysis combined with Common Sense Realism to become the scientific method of much nineteenth-century Protestantism and twentieth-century fundamentalism.

Conservatives such as Charles Hodge and B. B. Warfield believed that the Bible could be studied and *scientifically proven* to be valid. Out of this ethos, they developed the doctrine of Scripture known as inerrancy. Inerrancy's basic premise is that in the original autographs (*autographa*), the Bible was penned without human error. In other words, God left us an accurate, scientific record. Being a perfect historical document, the text was proof of divine inspiration. Based on this assumption, the Bible, as factual, could be demonstrated to be true. Hodge, armed with his premise that the Bible contained facts that were proof of divine inspiration, understood that the work of theologians and biblical scholars was not unlike the work of any other scientist. In the words of Hodge, the task of biblical scholars was to take the "truths" (facts) and "collect, authenticate, arrange, and exhibit them in their internal relation to each other."[25]

To return to Weber and the modern burden of disenchantment: for fundamentalist biblical science, the burden was one of scientific inquiry, of gathering facts that provided proof that the Bible was indeed true. As with its liberal counterpart, fundamentalist biblical studies became a disenchanted science. Within the fundamentalist version of the Bible, there now was no room for the supernatural or the mysterious. Such things left the face of the earth with the death of the apostles. In fact, conservatives disdained the supernatural just as much as, if not more than, the so-called secularists did!

24. See Keith Lehrer, "Epistemology: Thomas Reid on Truth, Evidence, and First Principles," *Canadian Journal of Philosophy* 41, no. S1 (2014): 155–66.

25. Charles Hodge, *Systematic Theology* (London: James Clarke, 1960), 1:1–2. In applying his direct and commonsense reading of the Bible, Hodge became a leading apologist for the institution of slavery.

In the same year as Weber's Munich lectures, Warfield delivered the Thomas Smyth Lectures at Columbia Theological Seminary. He titled these lectures "Counterfeit Miracles," and they were later developed into a book under the same name. Just as Weber placed the burden of disenchantment on science students, Warfield attempted to rid seminary students of any sense of the supernatural world. He warned these future ministers against "heathen modes of thought." Warfield lamented that Athanasius's *Life of Anthony* had such a romantic effect on Christianity. It was not more than a wedding of the fervor of Christian faith with Egyptian superstition. Leaving no supernatural stone unturned, Warfield noted that the miracles associated with St. Francis and other medieval monks reflected the "ingrained belief in magic which tinged the thought of an age so little instructed in the true character of the forces of nature."[26] In Warfield's estimation, Scripture was the infallible witness to Christ. It was the perfect historical witness, a scientific record of truth.[27]

Warfield's Christianity needed no more miracles. It had the record of miracles past. It needed no more mystery or deep clouds of God's presence. It had the perfect record of that in time past. The modern Christian was to look at the historical record, believe it, and follow its precepts. There was no enchanted space in Warfield's Christianity. Who needed enchantment when the Bible was a factual, accurate, and perfect historical record? In the words of Josh McDowell, a late twentieth-century Christian apologist, the Bible presented "evidence that demands a verdict."[28]

Warfield's vision of Christianity and the Bible had great influence over conservative Christianity. Many conservatives joined their vision of the Bible to dispensational theology (another loose form of Common

26. B. B. Warfield, *Counterfeit Miracles* (Edinburgh: Banner of Truth Trust, 1918), 66.

27. In 2008, ninety years after Warfield lectured at Columbia Theological Seminary, I was invited to deliver the Smyth Lectures. I chose the title "Pentecost and the Re-enchantment of the World"; sections of these lectures are woven into the fabric of this book. I have often humorously referred to the lectures as my "B. B. Warfield Take-Down."

28. Josh McDowell, *Evidence That Demands a Verdict*, vol. 1, *Historical Evidences for the Christian Faith* (Nashville: Nelson, 1979).

Sense Realism). Dispensational theology argued that history could be divided into seven dispensations or ages. These ages reveal God's "logic," his "science" for the plan of salvation. It's all in the science!

Over the course of a few decades, the landscape of early twentieth-century Christianity became disenchanted and hyperrational. Under the banner of truth, people learned to bear the great burden of disenchantment as the only reasonable means of preserving the faith. The emphasis on rationality and "objective science" continued throughout most of the last century.

Wilbert W. White's "Third Way"

At the height of the liberal-fundamentalist wars, Wilbert W. White (1863–1944), founder of Biblical Seminary in New York City (renamed New York Theological Seminary in 1966), attempted to pave a third way. White is best known as the father of the inductive method of Bible study. With its emphasis on close analysis of the biblical text in the vernacular, inductive Bible study was a means of empowering laity to do their own direct study. From Biblical Seminary, inductive study spread around the world; it became a transforming force in Christianity.

Among the graduates of Biblical Seminary is Eugene Peterson. Reflecting on his time there (1954–1957), Peterson recalled, "The seminary strategy . . . was not an abstract formula; it was basically an immersion in the biblical revelation in our mother tongue, incarnated in students and professors who composed what seems to me now, in retrospect, a unique minority ethos comprising common prayer in the chapel, common meals in the refectory, and common play."[29]

Inductive Bible study found a home among groups that had a love for the Bible but were not comfortable with fundamentalism's highly deductive approach to the text. In the spring of 2010 I spent

29. Remarks by Eugene Peterson, Annual Alumni/ae Day program, New York Theological Seminary, 2006; quoted in a letter to friends of New York Theological Seminary, October 22, 2018, https://www.nyts.edu/wp-content/uploads/2018/10/Peterson-2018-further-revised-ACM-Edit.pdf.

a sabbatical in the library at Union Theological Seminary reading through the Wilbert White archives. Having been a student of inductive Bible study and someone who had taught the method for over twenty-five years, I was interested in exploring how White's approach to the Bible both expressed and critiqued the modernity of his era.

I discovered that White was ahead of his time and, for that reason, was misunderstood and underappreciated. White's writing contained an ontological vision of the Bible that may be described as a place of real presence brought about by a robust pneumatology. Over the years, through the influence of subsequent leaders in the movement, inductive Bible study drifted away from White's original vision, becoming more rational, less open, less creative, and less pneumatic.[30] For that reason, White is better known for his approach to studying the Bible than for his beliefs about the nature of the Bible.

While holding to a scientific approach to the Bible, White rejected much of the rationalism found in both the liberal and conservative camps. As a student at Yale Divinity School, White studied with William Rainey Harper. Reflecting on his time with Harper, White wrote, "He inoculated me against the extremes of the Higher Criticism. I have its values, I believe, without its acridities." Harper also helped save White from "the disease itself (in spite of the inoculation) by his discovery of the need of a knowledge of the Bible itself in the mother tongue on the part of the ministry, and his ardent advocacy of the supply of this need especially by teaching the English Bible by books."[31]

Speaking of the battle between fundamentalists and modernists, White wrote, "These two minority groups long enough have claimed to be the only occupants of the field. They have tried to make us think that it is a field we are in, and that it is a battlefield instead of a highway. They have told us that we are compromisers and cowards; occu-

30. In an effort to bring inductive Bible study back to its earlier vision, Jackie David Johns and I coauthored *Encountering the Living Word: Relational Inductive Bible Study* (Marion, IN: Aldersgate, forthcoming).

31. Wilbert W. White, "Fourteen Points concerning Present Day Theological Education," June 1, 1932, private papers of Wilbert W. White, The Burke Library Archives, Union Theological Seminary.

piers of no-man's land if we decline to be on one side or the other."[32] In order to move from the battlefield to the highway, White proposed a "Word Way," a way that entailed dialectical tension among Word, church, and human reason. He saw this dialectical tension as the future of Bible study.

White's ecclesiology was expansive. He understood the church as including "the company of God's worshipers in times before Christ as well as since the Christian era began. The church began to be before the Old Testament began to be, and Christ heralded the good news of the Old Testament before the New Testament began the Bible." The church and the Bible are organically related. "The church produced the Bible and . . . the Bible produced the church. Neither existed without the other. Both came through the operation of the Spirit of God upon and through human personality."[33]

White advocated for the use of reason—reason that is enlightened and empowered by the Holy Spirit. "So we have the church, the Bible, and reason, in vital relationship, all under the influence of the Spirit of God. Thus we find that in a real sense, the author of the Bible is the Spirit of God. It follows that He is the interpreter of it. Thinking of the highest kind is called for in understanding the Bible. This kind of thinking is not inconsistent with the personal, direct overshadowing of the Spirit of God. It is in fact only possible in fellowship with the Eternal."[34]

White's vision of the Bible was thoroughly pneumatic. The Holy Spirit gave the Bible its supernatural dimension. He wrote, "The offense of the Bible always has been the presence in it of the supernatural. This supernatural element in the Bible is its strength; its

32. Wilbert W. White, "Two Minority Groups and Their Functions," January 22, 1931, private papers of Wilbert W. White, The Burke Library Archives, Union Theological Seminary.

33. Wilbert W. White, "The Future of Bible Study," August 14, 1910, Moganshan, China, private papers of Wilbert W. White, The Burke Library Archives, Union Theological Seminary.

34. Wilbert W. White, "What Is the Supreme Court of Appeal in Christianity? The Bible, the Church, Reason," n.d., private papers of Wilbert W. White, The Burke Library Archives, Union Theological Seminary.

super-reasonableness, not its unreasonableness, is its glory."[35] For White, the Bible contained real presence. In a tract titled "Pentecost—The Real Presence," White wrote, "The Real Presence—Do we not grasp it—this mystery of Pentecost? Is it not this?" Drawing from the words of John the Baptist, White asked, "Is not this baptism, the blessed and continuous oncoming and incoming of the Real Presence?"[36]

Unlike his contemporaries, White refused to make the Bible the first principle. In line with the historic creeds, he understood that faith began with God's revelation in Jesus Christ. Writes White, "A distinguished, eloquent and devoted minister of the Gospel in New York City announced as his subject for Sunday, October 19th, 1930, this thesis: 'The supreme issue today is the infallibility and inerrancy of the Bible.' I beg most courteously but most earnestly to submit that the supreme issue is rather the infallibility and inerrancy of our Lord and Savior Jesus Christ." White went on to say that the trouble with the doctrine of inerrancy was not the argument as much as its premise and its "absurd conclusion." He believed this doctrine laid a burden on Christianity that neither "we nor our fathers were able to bear." This burden resulted in "making orthodoxy synonymous with ignorance."[37]

White used ontological language to describe his alternative to inerrancy: "The Bible is both container and thing contained. It is both carrier and thing carried. . . . It is perfect for the purpose for which it has been given. Let all Christians beware and not stop with the Bible, but let it bring them to the Lord of life. This is its mission."[38]

White was hopeful for the future of Bible study. "The time is coming when the tendency of the scientific mind to be anti-supernatural

35. Wilbert W. White, "The Divine Library—Its Abuse and Use or How to Study the Bible," n.d., private papers of Wilbert W. White, The Burke Library Archives, Union Theological Seminary.

36. Wilbert W. White, "Pentecost—The Real Presence," tract 114, American Tract Society, New York, 1930.

37. Wilbert W. White, "'The Canon (The Bible) or Christ': Who? Or What?," 1930, private papers of Wilbert W. White, The Burke Library Archives, Union Theological Seminary.

38. White, "'The Canon (The Bible) or Christ': Who? Or What?"

will disappear. . . . As the humanness of the Scriptures is more and more recognized, their true divinity will be more deeply felt. There is the presence of God's part and of man's. The two cannot be separated." He saw the future as involving the humility of the inductive spirit found in the sciences with the humility necessary to enter the kingdom of God. The future of Bible study would be cautious and patient, willing to wait, being satisfied for a time "with the uncorrelated fragments of truth."[39]

Going through those dusty boxes of White's writings, I fell in love with inductive Bible study for the second time. My first love was rooted in my time as a graduate student at Wheaton College. This second love was rooted in discovering White's Pentecostal, sacramental reading of the Bible, which gave words to my own reading.

Pentecostalism's Uneasy Alliance with Fundamentalist Science

Even though Pentecostalism arrived on the scene at the height of the modern project, it did not fit into any of the modern categories of religion. Jackie Johns writes, "Pentecostalism was born outside of the dominant theological visions of the Christian world: nineteenth-century liberalism and reactionary fundamentalism." Furthermore, he says, "It was not the product of a scientific paradigm. Pentecostalism emerged simultaneously among a variety of peoples around the world. There were no theorists who constructed Pentecostalism as a plausible response to the failures of other systems."[40]

As a new movement, Pentecostalism did not have a body of scholars to help it theologically reflect on its experiences. Because the movement was regarded with suspicion, there were few theological dialogue partners. Fundamentalists saw Pentecostals as a dangerous sect. Mainline Protestants viewed them primarily through the lens

39. White, "Future of Bible Study."

40. Jackie Johns, "Pentecostalism and the Postmodern Worldview," *Journal of Pentecostal Theology* 3, no. 7 (January 1995): 84, 85.

of the social sciences, defining them as people who, uprooted from agrarian soil, sought solace in ecstatic religion.

For these reasons, Pentecostal theology developed as a hodgepodge, pulling together work from fundamentalist and Evangelical scholars. As Pentecostals established Bible schools and colleges, this movement's leaders organized the curriculum around the standard divisions: biblical studies, theological studies, and practical theology. During the early part of the twentieth century, Pentecostals found few choices for textbooks. At that time the standard conservative texts were basically fundamentalist; all were cessationist—meaning they believed that the gifts and operations of the Holy Spirit ceased at the end of the apostolic age. As the movement spread around the world, Pentecostal missionaries used fundamentalist texts in their Bible colleges. These fateful choices planted the seeds of fundamentalism within a movement that was, in its initial years, decidedly anti-fundamentalist.[41] As a result, Pentecostals developed an uneasy relationship with their own experiences of God. They learned to "filter" through books, editing when they found beliefs contrary to their own relationship with God. In particular, when it came to the Bible Pentecostals learned to live with a great deal of cognitive dissonance. On the one hand, their experience of the Bible was that of a living document, filled with the power and presence of God. On the other hand, their textbooks advocated for the scientific readings of Warfield and Hodge. The best identity they could carve out was "Fundamentalist plus" or "Evangelical plus." But by this they merely meant that, for them, the Bible was in reality the Word of God. They were not apologists for fundamentalism grounded in the Enlightenment.

During the latter part of the twentieth century, among Pentecostal scholars, especially those situated at the Church of God School of Theology (later Pentecostal Theological Seminary, Cleveland, TN), the cognitive dissonance between faith experienced and faith taught

41. See Harvey Cox, *Fire from Heaven: The Rise of Pentecostalism and the Reshaping of Religion in the Twenty-First Century* (Boston: Addison-Wesley, 1994). Cox gives an excellent comparison of Pentecostalism and fundamentalism.

began to give way. My husband, Jackie Johns, and I were part of this group, which became known as the Cleveland School of Pentecostal theology. Most of us were younger scholars who had been trained in both Evangelical and mainline schools, where we were given a freedom our elders had not been given—namely, freedom to explore our own identity as Pentecostals. Members of the Cleveland School began to ask, "Is there a particular hermeneutic of the Spirit?"[42] "Is there such a thing as a Pentecostal reading of Scripture?" This move toward confessional identity offered its own set of struggles; yet we pushed forward toward a more confessional stance of drinking from our own wells.[43]

The decades since the 1980s have included productive discussions on a Pentecostal worldview and reading of Scripture. As Robby Waddell notes, "Discussions concerning hermeneutics have preoccupied Pentecostal scholars for decades."[44] In these discussions, the question of the ontological nature of the Bible has taken a back seat to the hermeneutical quest. For the most part, discussions surrounding the nature of the Bible and ways to read the biblical text have been intra-Pentecostal.[45] It has been healthy to talk with and among ourselves. These discussions have been "iron sharpening iron," inasmuch as they have helped clarify issues of reading the Bible through a Pentecostal lens. However, the rest of Christianity struggles to come to terms

42. Father Francis Martin presented a paper at the 1984 meeting of the Society for Pentecostal Studies, "Spirit and Flesh in the Doing of Theology," in which he posed the question, "Is there a particular hermeneutic of the Spirit?"

43. See Gerald Sheppard, "Pentecostals and the Hermeneutics of Dispensationalism: The Anatomy of a Relationship," *Pneuma: The Journal of the Society for Pentecostal Studies* 16 (January 1984): 121–41.

44. Robby Waddell, "Hearing What the Spirit Says to the Churches: Profile of a Pentecostal Reader of the Apocalypse," in *Pentecostal Hermeneutics: A Reader*, ed. Lee Roy Martin (Leiden: Brill, 2013), 181.

45. The work of James K. A. Smith would be an exception to the intra-Pentecostal dialogue regarding hermeneutics. In *The Fall of Interpretation: Philosophical Foundations for a Creational Hermeneutic* (Downers Grove, IL: InterVarsity, 2000), Smith offers a creational hermeneutic of Scripture. He notes that this reading of the Bible is also "rather 'Pentecostal,' creating a space where there is room for a plurality of God's creatures to speak, sing and dance in a multivalent chorus of tongues" (20). Later in this book I will discuss how Smith offers an enchanted Pentecostal vision of nature as well as a Pentecostal approach to epistemology. Smith's work is foundational to this text.

with ways to read the Bible in a vastly different landscape than the one that existed a hundred years ago. Perhaps it is now time to offer our discussions to the larger body of Christ. This book is, in part, my attempt to do so. We are all facing the same cultural landscape and the ever-growing silence of the Bible, at least in the West.

Postmodernity and the Quest for the Bible

As scholars began to question modernity's claims to "objective reality" and the power of the rational human subject to know the world, they paved the way for a new era to emerge, one that is often called "postmodernity." This era has exposed the tyranny of systems of thought that seek to prove a certain vision of reality. James K. A. Smith writes, "First, postmodernism calls into question the supposed neutrality and universality of reason as proclaimed by the moderns. . . . Second, beyond merely pointing out the reductionist nature of Enlightenment 'rationality' and the veiled particularity of modernity's feigned universal reason, postmodernism actually *re*values embodiment and particularity."[46]

In many ways, postmodernity opens a door for the re-enchantment of the Bible. It allows for human experience to once again be a factor in biblical interpretation; it gives space for mystery and wonder. But postmodernity has its limits. The human subject continues to find it hard to divest its powers to name and objectify the world. As Taylor observes, "A certain awe still surrounds reason as a critical power, capable of liberating us from illusion and blind forces in instinct, as well as the fantasies bred of our fear and narrowness and pusillanimity."[47] This underlying awe at the power of critical reasoning and the hypercritical ability to deconstruct the tyrannies of modern systems of thought create an atmosphere of what may be called "hypermodernity."

46. James K. A. Smith, *Thinking in Tongues: Pentecostal Contributions to Christian Theology* (Grand Rapids: Eerdmans, 2010), 57.

47. Taylor, *Secular Age*, 9.

Deconstruction of the modern temples of reason, while holding on to the power of critical reason, has led to deconstruction itself becoming an endless process. "Wrenching things apart and breaking them up is more attractive for contemporary sensibility than hierarchically subsuming things under principles of order," writes Nathan Scott.[48] Scott draws from Mikhail Bakhtin's sense of carnival, a time in which "life (is) drawn out of its *usual* rut, . . . turned inside out,"[49] to identify the postmodern era of carnival as one in which nothing is given privileged status and everything is relativized. Such a world creates a sense of Babel, an irreversible hermeneutical situation of endless interpretations and meanings.[50] At its extreme end, the postmodern carnival becomes an endless fun house with no entrance and no exits, what Mark Taylor describes as "mazing grace."[51]

Caught in the endless maze of world making, the Bible can easily become merely one form of meaning among many. As the subject of endless forms of interpretation, each one attempting to destroy or have power over the other, Scripture's power to offer a way of "amazing grace" is diminished. Clearly, in order to deliver the Bible from its fate as the object of endless and competing meanings, we must move beyond hermeneutics into a very different space.

48. Nathan A. Scott Jr., "The House of Intellect in an Age of Carnival: Some Hermeneutical Reflections," *Journal of the American Academy of Religion* 55, no. 1 (Spring 1987): 4–5.

49. Mikhail Bakhtin, *Rabelais and His World*, trans. Helene Iswolsky (Bloomington: Indiana University Press, 1984), 122, as quoted in Scott, "House of Intellect," 6.

50. Scott, "House of Intellect," 7.

51. Mark Taylor, *Erring: A Postmodern A/theology* (Chicago: University of Chicago Press, 1984), chap. 7.

2

The Search for a Way Ahead

After years of adapting the Bible to modern sensibilities, Christians find themselves alienated from one another and, even worse, strangers to the biblical text. Forced to bear the burden of disenchantment, they have struggled to honor a text that has been stripped of its mysterious and sacred nature as Holy Scripture. Most contemporary Christians feel guilty for not reading the Bible. But the Bible does not seem to have enough power to draw people into its textual landscape.

Contemporary conservative Christians are told that they need to have a biblical worldview. Ironically, they are also warned to eschew the worldview of the Bible, meaning its profound mystery and deep presence in the Word of God. The modern version of the Bible offered to them has ceased to be a wonder-filled, sacred book. Therefore, it should be no surprise that its words have fallen on deafened ears.

At present, the question looming over the Christian church is this: Without returning to a precritical era, how do we re-enchant this text, making it once again a source of life, a light for the path of eternal life? This is a difficult question, but it is necessary because it addresses an urgent and pressing need in the life of Christian churches. We cannot abandon the Bible. As Eugene Peterson notes, "The Scriptures are the primary text for Christian spirituality. Christian spirituality is, in its entirety, rooted in and shaped by scriptural text."[1] If Christianity becomes devoid of its Scriptures, it will cease to be. Shaped by other practices, it will become something other than a "Christian" religion. Its adherents will cease to be "Christ-followers," since it is through the Bible that Jesus as the Living Word is revealed.

Protestants point to the Middle Ages, sometimes referring to it as the "Dark Ages," as an example of a time when the consequences of biblical illiteracy became apparent. While this period is often covered in broad brushstrokes that fail to see the presence of lively faith, the resulting portrait does contain elements of truth. The Bible was lost to the people of God. It was for the most part inaccessible, even to those who could read. However, we should also note that those who lived in the Middle Ages inhabited a world that was "Scripture-soaked": the Bible's stories, its messages, and its language permeated culture in visual art, poetry, music, and drama.

The silence of the Bible in contemporary Western civilization has more serious effects than was the case in centuries past. Within the larger culture, an ecology no longer exists that is permeated with Christian symbols, stories, and images. When the Bible goes silent among Christians in this context, the consequences can be especially devastating. Phyllis Tickle, in her assessment of the current silence of the Bible in the churches and in society, makes the point that the decline of biblical literacy is leading to a new generation of "scriptural innocents whose very ignorance is pushing them in one of two directions. Either innocence of scriptural experience is propelling them to seek ever more eagerly for structural engagement with it, or else a total lack of prior exposure is propelling Scripture itself farther and farther into the attics of life where all antiques are stored for a respectful period of time before being thrown completely away." For Tickle, neither scenario is healthy, for "naifs of every kind are

1. Eugene Peterson, *Eat This Book: A Conversation in the Art of Spiritual Reading* (Grand Rapids: Eerdmans, 2006), 15.

vulnerable at every turn, . . . easily exploited, easily crippled, easily sacrificed."[2]

Tickle makes an important and prophetic point. When biblical religion disappears, many false gods are waiting in the wings. Into the void of biblical illiteracy will come other texts, other images that will provide a template for living. One of the most powerful texts competing for Christian affections today is what Peterson calls "the text of the 'sovereign self.'"[3] The sovereign self is fed from the wells of consumption and acquisition.[4] The liturgies of commodification can trap us into thinking that the whole world and all who are in it are here for our pleasure. In this context, biblical illiteracy is especially toxic.

Alongside the cult of self-adoration is the enticing text of empire. This text is not new to human history. Throughout the ages, humankind has been attracted to the security and power of nationalism. Empires provide identity and security; at their best, they can lift up the ideals of justice, peace, equality, and freedom. Yet nationalism has a way of eclipsing Christian identity.

In today's increasingly frightening world, people look to empires whose "shock and awe" technology can ravish us with wonder and provide security. There is nothing unbiblical about patriotism, a love of one's country and its values. But since the days of Augustus Caesar, empire religion has never settled for being second place in our affections; it demands to be the center of life, scripting human discourse into the images of the "good life." Empire religion takes the affections, loyalties, and commitments that Christians should give to the kingdom of God and fuses them with patriotism. When this happens, the Bible becomes the script for national security and manifest destiny. It becomes the script for justification of unjust wars.

The time in which we live is especially precarious when it comes to empire religion. Mid-twentieth-century visions of the United Nations,

2. Phyllis Tickle, *The Great Emergence: How Christianity Is Changing and Why* (Grand Rapids: Baker Books, 2008), 116.

3. Peterson, *Eat This Book*, 32.

4. Cheryl Bridges Johns, "Cultivating a Heart for Holiness," *Enrichment* 16, no. 4 (Fall 2011): 35.

NATO, and the European Union are giving way to waves of nationalism. The image of the strong man seems more enticing than does conciliatory leadership and diplomacy. The nation-state led by a strong leader is now a compelling center of value and power for millions of Christians.

Following his book *The Strange Silence of the Bible in the Church*, James Smart wrote a sequel, *The Cultural Subversion of the Biblical Faith*. This disturbing and prophetic book explores the consequences of the Bible's silence in churches, particularly relative to the sociopolitical arena. "We have been afflicted all through this century with a peculiar blindness," notes Smart. "We had no difficulty in the 30s of recognizing the disastrous blindness of our fellow Christians in Germany who gave Hitler his opportunity—our evangelical fellow Christians, among them some distinguished theologians, even some who signed the Barmen Declaration. But when our own nations and their policies are concerned we can be equally blind and yet remain totally unconscious of it."[5]

The "cultural subversion of the biblical faith" should grieve us all. When we are held captive to a faith that relegates the biblical text to service of our various gods, then we have achieved idolatrous faith. Our prophetic witness in the world is diminished, and the presence of the Word of God becomes rare.

Beyond the Killing Fields of the Culture Wars

It may be that we are already well down the road of cultural subversion of the biblical faith. In the United States, Christians are engaged in bitter cultural wars. Both the religious right and the left are captive to certain visions of Christianity that are culturally scripted more than biblically narrated. In this context, the Bible is just a personal weapon and not a Word that comes from beyond us in true prophetic force.

5. James Smart, *The Strange Silence of the Bible in the Church: A Study in Hermeneutics* (Philadelphia: Westminster, 1970); Smart, *The Cultural Subversion of the Biblical Faith: Life in the Twentieth Century under the Sign of the Cross* (Philadelphia: Westminster, 1977), 9.

Wars have their victims; wars create orphans. Wars produce refugees as well as the tragically wounded. The culture wars are no exception. More than "collateral damage," our children, who looked for elders and found warriors, have become the real flesh-and-blood victims of these battles. They come from families torn apart by the shrill rhetoric of the prophets on the right and the left. These refugees from the culture wars are growing in number. They are the "postfundamentalists" or the "exvangelicals."

In 2017, the hashtags #exvangelical and #emptythepews filled the space of Twitter. These hashtags reflect how many young adults were choosing, and continue to choose, to leave behind the killing fields of their elders. Some of them left because of sexual abuse; others have abandoned the church due to the charged political climate. Like all refugees, they have stories to tell of their leaving, as well as hopes and dreams of a new land. Some of them have kept their Bibles but are searching for new ways to read this text, for "a textual hermeneutic that moves beyond the trench lines and polarizations of the mainline/evangelical cold war."[6] Others have abandoned their Bibles, equating Scripture with the culture from which they are fleeing.

We all deserve a Bible that beckons us to enter a wonderland where we encounter a living God who knows and loves us. We deserve a Bible that refuses to be co-opted in the service of culture wars. We deserve a Bible filled with the shock and awe of God's presence, to the degree that the glory offered by the empires of this world has no appeal. We deserve an enchanted text.

The Pressing Need for Re-enchantment

It is becoming increasingly clear that in the land that lies ahead, unless the Bible is reclaimed as Holy Scripture, the identity "Christian" will continue, but it will cease to reference a biblical religion. What is desperately needed today is a way of re-enchanting the Bible so that

6. Tim Conder and Daniel Rhodes, *Free for All: Rediscovering the Bible in Community* (Grand Rapids: Baker Books, 2009), 47.

we are ravished with wonder by both the beauty and the terror of the text, and by the shock and awe of a living God whose presence the Bible mysteriously reveals.

While there are those who are addressing the cultural captivity of the Bible, for the most part, these discussions fail to go beyond the modern reading of the Bible, continuing the liberal-conservative debate. In the end they offer little hope of re-enchanting the biblical text. These discussions can be divided into two camps: foundationalism and postfoundationalism.

Nancey Murphy defines foundationalism as "the theory of knowledge, based on the metaphor of knowledge as a building, that requires all beliefs to be justified by tracing them to a special category of beliefs that cannot be called into question."[7] Postfoundationalism is the search for some sort of middle ground between "beliefs that cannot be questioned" and nonfoundationalism's assertion that there is no such thing as an objective reality. For the foundationalist, truth is the objective building that everyone inhabits. For the postfoundationalist, truth is a communal gathering or a movable tent instead of a building.

Beyond a Biblical Worldview

The most prominent representative of the beliefs associated with foundationalism is commonly known as a "biblical worldview" or a "Christian worldview." The category of *worldview* is popular among many conservative Evangelicals, who see it as the answer to the cultural captivity of the Bible. Focus on the Family, a conservative Evangelical organization, defines a biblical worldview as "based on the infallible Word of God. When you believe the Bible is entirely true, then you allow it to be the foundation of everything you say and do."[8]

7. Nancey Murphy, *Beyond Liberalism and Fundamentalism: How Modern and Postmodern Philosophy Set the Theological Agenda* (New York: Continuum International, 2007), 2.

8. See Del Tackett, "What's a Christian Worldview?," Focus on the Family, January 1, 2006, https://www.focusonthefamily.com/faith/whats-a-christian-worldview/.

A 2003 Barna Group study is often cited as a resource for defining who does and does not qualify as having a "biblical worldview." Barna operationally defined a biblical worldview by using eight indicators:

1. Absolute moral truths exist.
2. The Bible defines these absolute moral truths.
3. Jesus Christ lived a sinless life during his ministry on earth.
4. God created the universe and continues to rule it today. He is omnipotent and omniscient.
5. Salvation is a gift from God. It cannot be earned through good works or behavior.
6. Satan is a real living entity.
7. Christians have an obligation to share the gospel with the unsaved.
8. The Bible is accurate in all its teachings.[9]

The list is as revealing in what it omits as in what it includes. The grand narrative of the Bible is reduced to eight concise statements that serve as a litmus test for defining orthodox biblical faith. Unlike the ancient creeds that begin with God, followed by narration of the story of salvation in Christ, this biblical worldview "creed" begins with "absolute moral truths exist" and then deduces other truths from there.

While these biblical worldview proponents are good at diagnosing the problems of scriptural illiteracy, they fail to offer a solution that gets at the heart of why people don't read and study the Bible. Biblical worldview ideology represents the height of Enlightenment thinking and modernity's emphasis on rationalism. Biblical worldview proponents fail to see how the Bible they offer is just another

9. Using these listed criteria, the results of surveying 2,033 adults were that only 4 percent of adults in the United States had a "biblical worldview." Barna Group, "A Biblical Worldview Has a Radical Effect on a Person's Life," December 3, 2003, https://www.barna.com/research/a-biblical-worldview-has-a-radical-effect-on-a-persons-life/.

modern version of truth-telling that is grounded in the idea that correct thinking is the key element of the Christian faith.

According to Barna, "People do not act like Jesus because they do not think like Jesus" (cf. Descartes, "I think, therefore I am").[10] In this line of reasoning, if people know the facts and/or principles of the Bible, they will, in turn, put those principles into action. This reductionist vision of humankind, which is as old as Plato, sees people as primarily thinking, rational beings. It leaves out the deep core affections that center the heart and drive our behavior in ways we cannot explain. Biblical worldview proponents fail to offer people a way of attending to the Bible that addresses their deep passions.

When the grand narrative of the Bible is reduced to a set of biblical principles that are propositionally distilled from the text, the human subject reigns supreme over the text, deducing its principles or laws and conceiving of ways to apply the truths of Scripture. This is not the same as abiding in the mysterious realm of sacred Word. It is not the same as having the Word of God alive in one's life so that the Bible becomes a habitation of the heart. It is not the same as "knowing" in the sense of the Hebrew term *yada*, which conveys an encounter with God resulting in a loving relationship.

At the present time, there is a pressing need to go beyond a biblical worldview as a solution to the problem of biblical illiteracy. It is becoming increasingly clear that the Bible must claim our affections as well as our minds. Our relationship with the Bible should bring about a deep passion for the kingdom of God that supersedes any other desire. The Bible should mark us with its power, naming us and branding us with its enchantments. That is does not is not the fault of the text itself. Rather, it is the fault of good people who, with the best intentions, have tamed and domesticated the text into a manageable reality so that it could be "better understood." This power over the text, in the end, has stripped it of its ability to capture us by its mysteries.

10. George Barna, *Think Like Jesus: Make the Right Decision Every Time* (Brentwood, TN: Integrity Publishing, 2003).

Beyond Postfoundationalism

In this strange transitional era that is somewhere between modernity and postmodernity, a common option for reading the Bible is postfoundationalism, sometimes known as postliberalism. Postfoundationalism's approach to the text understands belief systems to be culturally and linguistically formed. In this context, the Bible is understood as a catechetical, community-forming text. It frames the world for habitation and meaning. The Bible creates a "peculiar people" among those who read and live by the story of the text.[11]

While tentative on just how to read the Scriptures, proponents of postfoundationalism are certain that they do not understand the Bible as containing timeless propositional truths. They seek to re-envision the Bible as a living, communal document. In this sense, the Bible becomes the bread that is "free for all" within the context of a communal reading of the text. For Tim Conder and Daniel Rhodes, pastors at Emmaus Way in Durham, North Carolina, "A foundationalism that holds the possibility of a sacred, abstract Bible—a Bible that can exist as God's Word apart from the people to whom it was revealed as a gift—is on shaky ground." The Bible, they say, is "identified and received as a living Word . . . [that] demands the presence of faithful community to interpret and embody the texts."[12]

Rachel Held Evans offers another example of a postfoundational reading of the Bible. Her book *Inspired* resonated with a generation of exvangelicals who had, for the most part, left their Bibles behind. Evans writes, "The Bible of my twenties served only as a stumbling block, as a massive obstacle between me and the God I thought I knew." Eventually, Evans reclaimed the Bible, but it was not the Bible of her youth. The biblical text is *inspired*. But for Evans, "Inspiration is not about some disembodied ethereal voice dictating words or notes to a catatonic host. It's a collaborative process, a holy give-and-take, a

11. See Hans W. Frei, *The Eclipse of Biblical Narrative: A Study in Eighteenth and Nineteenth Century Hermeneutics* (New Haven: Yale University Press, 1980); William H. Willimon, *Peculiar Speech: Preaching to the Baptized* (Grand Rapids: Eerdmans, 1992).

12. Conder and Rhodes, *Free for All*, 62.

partnership between Creator and creator."[13] Evans invites her readers to pick up their Bibles again and find stories much like their own. The themes that emerge from the biblical narrative offer fresh, *inspired* visions for living today.

Within the postliberal reading of the Bible, there is a haunting missing element: the Bible as Holy Scripture. Postliberalism retains the human subject over the text as the final arbiter of truth, even though it places the subject within the context of community. The community of subjects continues the hermeneutical turn that relegated the text to the status of object.

In postfoundational readings of the text, there is the ever-present danger of textual tribalism—each group having its own narrative and reading of the biblical text without any norming standard of biblical interpretation. Such is the irony of late modernity—celebrating human otherness while denying the otherness of the biblical text. The Bible is a text that helps shape ecclesial communal identity. In this sense, Conder and Rhodes's understanding of the Bible as a community-forming text is helpful in showing how the Bible can function in this constructive manner. On the other hand, McClure says, the Bible *as Scripture* "refuses over and over again to close itself as a book, to secure its connotations to a single self-referential tautology."[14]

To sum it all up, postfoundationalism does not help toward re-enchanting the Bible. By giving the community final say, it removes the power of "Word." No community can replicate the power of revelation in its convicting and life-transforming force. The community can testify to the Word, but only in a way that is secondary and interpretative.

Whether we are in the camp of foundationalism or of postfoundationalism, the Bible has become a book that, in the words of Walter Brueggemann, speaks in "cadences that sound strangely like our

13. Rachel Held Evans, *Inspired: Slaying Giants, Walking on Water, and Loving the Bible Again* (Nashville: Nelson, 2018), xvii, xxiii.

14. John S. McClure, *Other-Wise Preaching: A Postmodern Ethic for Homiletics* (St. Louis: Chalice, 2001), 21.

own."[15] It has become a text that describes our world and not one that has the power to disrupt, redescribe, or reorient it.

I believe that most people hunger for a different Bible than what is currently being offered by those advocating either foundationalist or postfoundationalist readings of the text. We all hunger for a new textual reality wherein the text comes alive as a multidimensional world that beckons us into its mysteries. This hunger is found among Christians of all stripes. The answer lies beyond the trenches of the culture wars. It is found in our discovery of the Bible as a sacred, dangerous, mysterious, and presence-filled wonderland. Unless we find the depth of this text, the rate of biblical illiteracy will increase, and the post-Christian landscape will continue to expand.

15. Walter Brueggemann, *The Word That Redescribes the World: The Bible and Discipleship* (Minneapolis: Fortress, 2006), 6.

3

Longing for Enchantment

> I want so badly to believe
> That there is truth, that love is real.
>
> —The Postal Service, "Clark Gable"[1]

Despite our forebears' heroic attempts to accommodate to the burden of disenchantment, people living in the twenty-first century express a growing hunger for mystery and a greater openness to things once dismissed as naive and superstitious. We are living in a period that Max Weber could not have imagined. In an interview with National Public Radio, Adam Frank observed that Weber's fears of an "iron cage" of modern systems of efficiency and control have not materialized. Frank noted, "On a more intimate level the disenchantment that was also to be our fate never made it to its full tyranny. Just as the human world as a whole was growing colder and more machine-like, individuals kept finding ways to create vitality and wonder, like grass growing up from cracks in the pavement."[2]

1. I am indebted to James K. A. Smith for these song lyrics. See his lecture "From Excarnation to Re-enchantment: Why Imagination Is Crucial for Mission," Dallas Theological Seminary, November 2, 2018, https://voice.dts.edu/chapel/from-excarnation-to-re-enchantment/.

2. Adam Frank, "Beyond Science vs. Religion: Re-Enchanting the World," *Cosmos & Culture* 13.7 (blog), September 21, 2010, https://www.npr.org/sections/13.7/2010/09/21/130015634/-beyond-science-vs-religion-re-enchanting-the-world.

These days there seems to be a lot of enchantment growing through the cracks in the paved-over world of modernity. Enchantment can be seen in domains of science as well as religion. In 2006 I was asked to be part of a gathering of scientists and Evangelicals to discuss the crisis of global climate change. This meeting was my awakening to how much the old barriers between faith and science might not be as tight as we have imagined them to be.

The two-day meeting—held at Melhana, a rural plantation in Georgia—was the brainchild of an unlikely partnership between Richard Cizik and Eric Chivian. At that time, Cizik served as vice president for governmental affairs for the National Association of Evangelicals. Chivian was a Nobel laureate and director of the Center for Health and the Global Environment at Harvard Medical School. Cizik and Chivian envisioned a gathering of about twenty Evangelical leaders and scientists to form a partnership in addressing climate change as well as the ways humans were contributing to the rapid decline of many plant and animal species. They knew that such a gathering was fraught with opportunities for conflict and that it had the potential to dissolve into a combative event. For that reason, they consulted with an expert in conflict resolution before the meeting.

Everyone who attended this gathering came with a great deal of anxiousness. For the most part, it was a secret gathering. A couple of Evangelicals insisted that no one would know they were there. What if people found out that they were talking about global climate change, and even worse, meeting with secular scientists, some of whom were atheists? The scientists had their own reputations to consider. "I must admit I approached that meeting with some anxiety," said Chivian. "I'm involved in evolutionary biology. I support stem-cell research."[3]

Being the only Pentecostal in the room, I feared that both scientists and Evangelicals would reject me. To say that I went with anxiety is an understatement.

3. Billy Baker, "Saving 'God's Creation' Unites Scientist, Evangelical Leader," *Boston Globe*, May 1, 2008, http://archive.boston.com/news/local/massachusetts/articles/2008/05/01/saving_gods_creation_unites_scientist_evangelical_leader/.

Not one of us could have dreamed of what actually happened. The first evening of our gathering, we sat in a circle, each of us eyeing the others with suspicion. I imagine the scientists half expected some of us to have large KJV Bibles in our laps. The leaders began the meeting by asking each of us to share our love for the creation. As we told our stories, the palatable tension began to melt. During the course of sharing our love for the earth and our concern for its future, our disparate lives—as atheists, Christians, theologians, and scientists—were mysteriously woven into a united tapestry of "deep, fundamental commitment to life on earth."[4]

At the end of the evening we all sat stunned, unable to fully grasp what had transpired. I remember looking at these Nobel- and Pulitzer Prize–winning scientists with new eyes. They loved what I loved. They saw what I saw. And they knew what I needed to know: just how deep we were into the possibility of losing much of the world's habitat.

In the next couple of days, there were times when I sensed what Rudolf Otto described as the *mysterium tremendum* weighing down upon our gathering.[5] This mysterious presence carried a sense of urgency that was hard for anyone to describe. One afternoon, while I was on a walk, a scientist of the Intergovernmental Panel on Climate Change of the United Nations stopped me. He had tears in his eyes. "I didn't realize my work had spiritual implications," he said.

From this unprecedented meeting, the Scientists and Evangelicals Initiative for the care of creation was formed. We issued a joint statement urging immediate action to slow the speed of climate change and the destruction of the earth's fragile ecology. "We agree that our home, the Earth, which comes to us as that inexpressibly beautiful and mysterious gift that sustains our very lives, is seriously imperiled by human behavior," reads the statement.[6] (It was the scientists who

4. Baker, "Saving 'God's Creation.'"

5. Rudolf Otto, *The Idea of the Holy: An Inquiry into the Non-rational Factor in the Idea of the Divine and Its Relation to the Rational*, trans. John Harvey (London: Oxford University Press, 1926), 12.

6. "An Urgent Call to Action: Scientists and Evangelicals Unite to Protect Creation," National Press Club, Washington, DC, January 17, 2007, https://www-tc

insisted on the words "beautiful and mysterious gift" being added to our document.)

Most of the scientists I encountered at this historic meeting had, and have, an enchanted vision of creation. Even though many of them profess not to believe in God, they approach their work with wonder, awe, and a keen awareness that the universe is profoundly beautiful and mysterious. Their commitment to serving and protecting the earth's most vulnerable—its tiny creatures as well as the poor—set them apart from the radical New Atheists, a group known for their disdain of Christianity.[7]

Scientists and Evangelicals uniting in their love for creation is only one example of a place where enchantment is growing. If we are careful to pay attention, we can see that signs of re-enchantment are everywhere: Francis Collins finding God as he mapped the human genome,[8] the popularity of the Lord of the Rings and Harry Potter series of books and movies, and the return to more ancient forms of spirituality. When Yo-Yo Ma picked up his cello at home and recorded "Songs of Comfort" for a world caught in the grip of a major pandemic, he gave us enchanted music that calmed our fears.

James K. A. Smith describes the contemporary longing for enchantment as a "haunting." He uses the words of British novelist

---

.pbs.org/now/shows/343/letter.pdf. From this initial gathering, several joint projects resulted, including a trip to an island off the coast of Alaska to witness firsthand the drastic effects of climate change. Some members joined together to host meetings on university campuses. I hosted a meeting at Lee University, a Pentecostal institution. Scientists who joined me included Carl Safina, founder of the Blue Ocean Institute, and Nobel laureate Paul Epstein. The friendships formed at that remote location in Georgia continue to this day.

7. For a good analysis of the intolerance of the New Atheists, see Ted Davis and Stephen Snobelen, "Francis Collins and the Intolerance of the New Atheists," BioLogos, March 8, 2017, https://biologos.org/articles/francis-collins-and-the-intolerance-of-the-new-atheists. The world-renowned scientist E. O. Wilson was present at the gathering of scientists and Evangelicals. Although he had long abandoned a belief in God, he was markedly different from the New Atheists in his attitude toward Christians. A few months before the Melhana meeting, Wilson wrote *The Creation: An Appeal to Save Life on Earth* (New York: Norton, 2006), which was an attempt to reach out to conservative Christians with a plea for their participation in preserving creation.

8. See Francis Collins, *The Language of God: A Scientist Presents Evidence for Belief* (New York: Free Press, 2007).

Julian Barnes, the poster child of British secularization, to describe this haunting: "I don't believe in God, but I miss him."[9] This longing can also find expression in the words "I don't believe in miracles, but I miss them." Or, "I don't believe in the Bible, but I miss it." Writes Andrew Root, "We have a sense of being crossed up; we doubt what we long for. We doubt that what we long for is sensible. Almost all of us yearn for poetry instead of prose, for mystery over cold transparency, and yet we need to face the facts."[10]

The world is ripe for re-enchantment, yet I'm afraid too many Christians, especially the heirs of the Reformation, are missing this moment. After centuries of drinking the waters of disenchantment, Western Christians have become some of the most ardent defenders of the secularism that Charles Taylor describes as "excarnation": the "transfer of our religious life out of bodily forms of ritual, worship, practice, so that it comes more and more to reside 'in the head.'"[11] A rational view of faith as well as a "facts-and-principles Bible" are but two examples of Protestant excarnation.

The Haunting Landscape of the Age of Authenticity

Taylor describes the present secular era as the "Age of Authenticity," a time when "the understandings of human life, agency, and the good" are found in expressive individualism.[12] In this context, the drive for enchantment becomes an expression of individuality. Smith succinctly summarizes what Taylor is describing: "This is no longer a space of common action but rather a space of *mutual display*—another way of 'being-with' in which 'a host of urban monads hover on the boundary between solipsism and communication.'"[13]

9. Smith, "From Excarnation to Re-enchantment."

10. Andrew Root, *The Pastor in a Secular Age: Ministry to People Who No Longer Need a God* (Grand Rapids: Baker Academic, 2019), 30.

11. Charles Taylor, *A Secular Age* (Cambridge, MA: Harvard University Press, 2007), 613.

12. Taylor, *Secular Age*, 474.

13. James K. A. Smith, *How (Not) to Be Secular: Reading Charles Taylor* (Grand Rapids: Eerdmans, 2014), 86. See also Taylor, *Secular Age*, 482.

What forms might the search for enchantment take in the Age of Authenticity, a world of "mutual display"? One way of answering this question is to look at the modern carnival, places where people can, for a time, inhabit a world not governed by the dull routinization of modern living. In his reflections on the meaning of carnival, Taylor observes that "the call of anti-structure is still strong in our highly interdependent, technological, super-bureaucratized world. In some ways, [it is] more powerful than ever."[14]

Burning Man is one example of carnival in the Age of Authenticity. It uniquely combines the quest for self-expression and the play of anti-structure. Held annually in the Black Rock Desert of Nevada, the festival draws thousands of participants. In addition to the annual event, there is also the larger Burning Man community, which is supported by a website and local groups, as well as other forms of communication.

The Burning Man festival is a time for life to be "drawn out of its *usual* rut" or in some way "turned inside out."[15] Conventional hierarchical norms and structures are suspended, and "life is invaded by a great wave of riotous antinomianism."[16] Each year participants, called "burners," defy the extremes of the desert by building temporary shelters that serve not only to shield them from the heat but also to express some unique aspect of the theme of the festival. Burning Man is a celebration of art as well as a test of survival.

The festival began in 1986 when, at the time of the summer solstice, Larry Harvey and Jerry James decided to "burn the Man." They built a wooden effigy and burned it on a beach in San Francisco. In the following years, they continued the summer solstice custom of burning the Man, and crowds began to gather. In 1989, the effigy was forty feet high, and at that gathering members of the Cacophony Society

14. Taylor, *Secular Age*, 53.

15. Mikhail Bakhtin, *Rabelais and His World*, trans. Helene Iswolsky (Bloomington: Indiana University Press, 1984), 122.

16. Nathan A. Scott Jr., "The House of Intellect in an Age of Carnival: Some Hermeneutical Reflections," *Journal of the American Academy of Religion* 55, no. 1 (Spring 1987): 6.

joined the celebration. The Burning Man website notes, "This new group brought with it an underground ethos. This is when it began to be imagined as what Hakim Bey called an 'interzone'—a secret caravan oasis, a chink in the armor of society, a place where you can get in and get out, like some artistic Viet Cong, and get away with things. Bey had styled this 'poetic terrorism.'"[17] Since 1990, Nevada's Black Rock has served as the location for the "poetic terrorism" called Burning Man.

Burning Man is a unique gestalt of self-expression as well as community. It is carnival, in the sense that it suspends time and the norms of society. It offers the possibility of inhabiting an enchanted space where rules give way to creativity, nonconformity, and play. Since the early years, a large number of people who work in Silicon Valley have been part of Burning Man. The festival grants them a way of deconstructing the technological society they help create. In the words of Elon Musk, CEO of Tesla, Burning Man "is Silicon Valley."[18] In addition to Silicon Valley techs, Burning Man attracts people from all around the world. In 2019 over seventy-eight thousand people attended.

In spite of the rising number of burners, Burning Man is not a diverse community. Of the seventy-eight thousand participants in 2019, records show that 82.2 percent were White and that the median income was well over the national US average. These demographics may reflect how keenly a certain segment of Western culture feels the strange presence of absence, or what Taylor calls "the malaise of immanence." Notes Taylor, "Some people feel a terrible flatness in the everyday, and this experience has been identified particularly with commercial, industrial, or consumer society. They feel [the] emptiness of the repeated, accelerating cycle of desire and fulfillment in consumer culture; the quality of bright supermarkets, or neat row housing in a clean suburb."[19]

17. Burning Man Timeline, "1989: Saturday June 24th," Burning Man, https://burningman.org/timeline/1989.

18. Nick Bilton, "A Line Is Drawn in the Desert," *New York Times*, August 20, 2014, E1.

19. Taylor, *Secular Age*, 309.

The center of Burning Man continues to be the large wooden man who is burned on the final night of the festival. The Man is an icon for the community of burners. It represents "nothing expressed or explicable, yet it is a physical and ethical guidepost."[20] To those suffering from the malaise of immanence, Burning Man offers a stark form of enchantment. In many ways, it is an icon of the postmodern idea of transgression, a time of deconstruction and reconstruction, where boundaries are transgressed and redrawn, where social norms are transgressed and remade, over and over.[21]

In ages past, while it was a suspension of time and norms, the celebration of carnival was tied to history; it preceded Lent and Easter. Carnival offered temporary liminal space, a time to inhabit the tension between the expectations of a sacred world and the profane. In this sense, while carnival suspended the rules, it was still tied to a larger sacred ethos. Its riotous play gave way to the drama of the larger story of Lent and Easter. Until the modern era, carnival and the world outside of carnival were enchanted. In today's world, both carnival time and mundane time exist within the immanent frame of the natural world. When a Burning Man festival is over, the enchanting space of Black Rock Desert gives way to the mundane existence of modern technological society. Each year, the malaise of the technological world extinguishes the fires in the Black Rock Desert.

Burning Man expresses the haunting that surrounds the contemporary world, a haunting that reveals both a deep longing for enchantment and the inability to find it. This haunting can be seen in the ten core principles that guide the community: "radical inclusion, gifting, decommodification, radical self-reliance, radical self-expression, communal effort, civic responsibility, leaving no trace,

20. Burning Man Project, "What Is Burning Man? History and Timeline," https://burningman.org/about/history/brc-history/man-base/.

21. For a religious studies analysis of Burning Man, see Tio Lloyd, "Understanding Burning Man through Fundamental Religious Studies Theories," *Sound Ideas*, Summer Research (Summer 2020): 376, https://soundideas.pugetsound.edu/summer_research/376.

participation, and immediacy."[22] On the one hand, these principles speak of a longing for connection, a world in which things are gifted instead of commodified, a world of participation and communal effort, and a world in which humans do not deface the creation. On the other hand, the principles of "radical self-reliance" and "radical self-expression" reveal how burners are caught in the tension between their longing for deep connection and the hyperindividualism that characterizes the Age of Authenticity.

The Haunting of Protestantism

When Jackie and I took our daughter to college, we were given the opportunity to attend a meeting for the parents of entering students. It was a time for faculty and administrators to give parents an overview of the ethos of this Evangelical college as well as an opportunity to ask questions. One parent's question stands out in my memory. It went something like this: "We brought our daughter here as an Evangelical. We want her to stay an Evangelical, yet we have concerns about the large number of students and faculty who attend a charismatic Anglican church in the area. What is this school going to do to stop its students and faculty from leaving our faith?"

The question posed by this anxious parent expressed the views of generations of Evangelicals who understand their faith as separate from the "liturgical churches." In their minds, their ancestors had suffered to break free from the "magic" of the old churches and to lift up personal salvation as well as *sola scriptura*. They do not want their children lured back into captivity. The question may also be an expression of concern about the rising popularity of Pentecostal-Charismatic spirituality. Who wants their nice Evangelical daughter to go off the deep end into fanaticism?

Evangelical students entering college in 2005 most likely grew up in churches that were struggling with their own malaise of immanence.

22. Burning Man Project, "What Is Burning Man? The 10 Principles of Burning Man," https://burningman.org/about/10-principles/.

Many suburban Evangelical churches had already made the move to becoming "seeker friendly," operating out of buildings that looked more like shopping malls than cathedrals. Writes Andrew Root, "These new churches in suburban America were the height of secular: no time-bending gravity permeated their walls."[23] In these spaces, pastors were less like priests and more like entrepreneurs.

By the mid-twentieth century, the immanent frame of modernity, the assertion that lives should be primarily natural, was fast becoming a core part of the Evangelical world. Seeker-friendly churches seemed to be working hard at blocking out transcendence and any sense of the sacramental. The emphasis on meeting individual needs and programs facilitating "purpose-driven lives" made it difficult to imagine divine action.[24] Excarnation became normative.

Worship in many Evangelical churches, with its emphasis on entertaining an audience, has more the flavor of a rock concert than of a gathering where the people of God join together in the work of the liturgy. These churches fit nicely into the Age of Authenticity. People can have their individual experiences of God without even knowing the person standing next to them. The services are sprinkled with enchantment, just enough to create an environment of "praise and worship" without threatening the autonomous self. Some Evangelical churches maintain singing of traditional hymns, but the ethos of the worship has a decidedly rational and disembodied tone. For many years, whether one worshiped in seeker-friendly settings or in traditional contexts, no one seemed to notice or miss the presence of the divine in the material world—until they did.

Over the past few years, young Evangelicals have steadily been moving toward the sacramental spirituality of liturgical churches. Here they find grace communicated in ways that move beyond the starkly oral and disembodied forms of worship and move into the material world of bread, wine, oil, and the laying on of hands. Rachel Held Evans writes, "The sacraments drew me back to church after I'd

23. Root, *Pastor in a Secular Age*, 18–19.
24. Root, *Pastor in a Secular Age*, 21.

given up on it. When my faith became little more than an abstraction, a set of propositions to be affirmed or denied, the tangible, tactile nature of the sacraments invited me to touch, smell, taste, hear, and see God in the stuff of everyday life again."[25]

The haunting for enchantment among Evangelicals goes beyond a longing for incarnation. It also includes a hunger for deep rootedness in something larger than one's own specific church or denomination. Born at the crossroads of Protestant resistance to state churches and the fires of revival, US Evangelical churches have always had a loose connection to historical Christianity. In addition, the phenomenon of independent churches, those unmoored from denominational identity, is uniquely American. This sense of rootlessness has been exacerbated by the loss of connection that was once found by living one's whole life in a community where extended family and church interconnected.

In his foreword to Winfield Bevins's book *Ever Ancient, Ever New: The Allure of Liturgy for a New Generation*, Scot McKnight testifies of his own journey from mainstream Evangelicalism to Anglicanism. "I grew up in an autonomous church loosely connected to the Conservative Baptists, and I had no reason to break loose and join the Presbyterians or the Methodists or the Episcopals in my hometown." However, when McKnight moved to England, his family was invited to attend St. Peter's Church (Toton). Their family had never used The Book of Common Prayer, but when McKnight "heard for the first time the words of the collects, those weekly prayers recited, often from rote memory, [his] born-again past met the living faith of living words." Notes McKnight, "I was overwhelmed. And have been ever since."[26]

My own tradition, Pentecostalism, has always been an enchanted form of Christianity; in many places of the majority world, it continues to be so. Even as the world rushed toward secularization,

25. Rachel Held Evans, *Searching for Sunday: Loving, Leaving, and Finding the Church* (Nashville: Thomas Nelson, 2015), xvi.

26. Scot McKnight, foreword to Winfield Bevins, *Ever Ancient, Ever New: The Allure of Liturgy for a New Generation* (Grand Rapids: Zondervan, 2019), 12.

Pentecostals offered space "where the plausibility of the secular was suspended."[27] Incarnation was everywhere: in the laying on of hands, in anointing with oil, in the gifts of the Spirit operating among the people. In recent decades, Pentecostals in North America have gained entrance into the Evangelical world, but in doing so, they felt the pressure to leave behind some of the more extreme forms of enchantment.

Over the years, many Pentecostals have made peace with secularism, which can be seen in the little difference that exists between Pentecostal seeker-friendly churches and those within mainstream Evangelicalism. "Pentecostal light" may best describe the vibe of such churches, where the liturgy is more like a rock concert than the old-time religion. These days, people rarely fall out in the Spirit, and the gifts of prophecy and interpretation of tongues are decreasing. The most dramatic move is the shift in the focus of worship from the anointed congregation to the stage, where a celebrity pastor and a worship and praise team take the spotlight. Each Sunday, worshipers sit in darkened rooms, barely able to see anyone around them. The spotlight is on the stage.

Coming to the End of the Secular Age?

In his musings about the future of the secular age, Taylor lays out two alternative futures. One future sees religion shrinking further and further into the background. In this scenario, religion will not disappear completely. Rather, it will become an expression of minority opinions and quite marginal to society at large. The second scenario involves the awareness of transcendent reality achieving a broader consensus. The shutting out of this awareness may not be as severe as it is at the present time, but Taylor questions the degree to which people of the future will be open to the transcendent. He references the words of T. S. Eliot, "Human kind cannot bear much reality." Too much reality is often destabilizing, and "openness to transcendence is fraught with

27. Wolfgang Vondey, "Religion at Play: Pentecostalism and the Transformation of a Secular Age," *Pneuma* 40, no. 2 (2018): 18.

peril."[28] A greater openness to transcendence and lessening of the immanent frame "will intensify the sense of living in a 'waste land.'" In response to this awareness, "many young people will begin again to explore beyond the boundaries."[29] However, this exploration does not necessarily include finding a home where there are shared religious beliefs and where religious beliefs are tied to a social framework.

In her book *Strange Rites: New Religions for a Godless World*, Tara Isabella Burton describes "religious rituals of our so-called secular age: a place where faith and fantasy, art and irony, capitalism and creation converge." These rituals, Burton says, "are the holy of holies for the religiously unaffiliated—the fastest-growing religious demographic in America—the spiritual but not religious, the religious mix and matches, the theologically bi- and tri-curious who attend Shabbat services but also do yoga, who cleanse with sage but also sing 'Silent Night' at Christmastime. Throughout America, already the religiously unaffiliated make up about a quarter of the population and almost 40 percent of young millennials."[30]

Burton notes that we are not just watching the rise of the so-called Nones; we are also experiencing a whole new wave of religion, what she calls "religion remixed." Burton points out that this form of faith mirrors what Émile Durkheim described as a "collective effervescence." Burton describes this new religion as "quintessentially American, . . . a religion of emotive intuition, of aestheticized and commodified experience, of self-creation and self-improvement, and yes, selfies." It is "decoupled from institutions, from creeds, from metaphysical truth-claims about God or the universe or the Way Things Are, but [it] still seeks—in various and varying ways—to provide us with the pillars of what religion always has: meaning, purpose, community, ritual."[31]

Burton illustrates this new form of religion with a vivid description of the wildly popular immersive experience *Sleep No More*,

28. Taylor, *Secular Age*, 769
29. Taylor, *Secular Age*, 770.
30. Tara Isabella Burton, *Strange Rites: New Religions for a Godless World* (New York: Public Affairs, 2020), 2.
31. Burton, *Strange Rites*, 2–3.

which takes place in the McKittrick Hotel, located in New York City's Chelsea neighborhood. This space is "equal parts warehouse, performance art space, bar, and party venue."[32] Inside the hotel awaits the enchanted world of Shakespeare's *Macbeth*. Guests wear masks and are free to wander around the several floors of the old hotel, where every item and every space has meaning tied to the *Macbeth* narrative. Cast members interact with roving guests; the lucky guests may experience "a coveted, intimate, sometimes sexually charged encounter with a character" in the drama.[33]

Sleep No More has a faithful cult following. For the faithful, largely millennial New Yorkers, this immersive experience becomes part home, part church, and part therapy session. They come back, week after week, spending thousands of dollars for the opportunity to inhabit an enchanted space. Burton points out that immersive experiences such as *Sleep No More* mimic rituals and "mark the passing of time through a carnival atmosphere of transcendence. They [are] invitations . . . to enter this world of witchcraft and magic" and, for a short while, to celebrate the subversion of established societal norms.[34] It is Burning Man with an East Coast vibe. Just as burners torch the Man each year, returning everything to nothingness, the character of Hecate in *Sleep No More* lip-synchs Peggy Lee's "Is That All There Is?" In the end, for both Burning Man and *Sleep No More*, "the world is a fundamentally meaningless place: a random kaleidoscope of atoms and mistakes."[35]

Just as the invention of the printing press fueled the spread of the Reformation, Burton sees the internet fueling the new forms of remixed religion. It does seem that many postmoderns have come to the end of the book and are thus enticed to enter the way of the internet's "mazing grace,"[36] where they are free to remix their own religion.

32. Burton, *Strange Rites*, 1.
33. Burton, *Strange Rites*, 3.
34. Burton, *Strange Rites*, 6–8.
35. Burton, *Strange Rites*, 12.
36. Mark Taylor, *Erring: A Postmodern A/theology* (Chicago: University of Chicago Press, 1984), chap. 7.

In dialogue with Mark Taylor, James K. A. Smith offers his own possibilities for the future:

> Evangelicals who have been raised and shaped by forms of Christianity that are "roughly fundamentalist" will either:
>
> a. become taken with the modern moral order and thus sort of replay the excarnational development of modernity, just now a few centuries later, sort of catching up with the wider culture; so under the guise of the "emerging church" or "progressive" evangelicalism, we'll be set on a path to something like Protestant liberalism, a new deism; or
> b. recognize the disenchantment and excarnation of evangelical Protestantism, and also reject the Christianized subtraction stories of liberal Christianity, and feel the pull of more incarnational spiritualities, and thus move toward more "Catholic" expressions of faith—and these expressions of faith will actually exert more pull on those who have doubts about their "closed" take on the immanent frame.[37]

To Smith's two options, I would add a third: what Burton identifies as a strident, nonreligious form of fundamentalism. This fundamentalism can take two expressions: either a disenchanted model of social justice or a disenchanted form of social preservation. Burton identifies the new generation of social justice warriors as being unmoored from religious beliefs. Compared to the national average of Americans, this group is "more than twice as likely to say that they 'never pray.'" They are less likely than their social gospel predecessors to quote Scripture, and they do not attend religious services. They are "twice as likely to have finished college, and about three times more likely to say they're 'ashamed to be an American.'" Politics is "an integral part of their identity."[38] Alexandria Ocasio-Cortez, a member of the House of Representatives for New York, is the icon for this movement.[39]

37. Smith, *How (Not) to Be Secular*, 138–39.

38. Burton, *Strange Rites*, 170.

39. For more on the notion of individuals serving as icons for a particular cultural moment, see Burton, *Strange Rites*, 169–89.

Some exvangelicals find the social justice culture appealing because it offers what they see missing in their former churches: justice, equality, and a vision of an enchanted world where everyone is loved and welcomed. Where once they were born-again believers and welcomed into the arms of the church, now they are becoming "woke" and welcomed into the arms of a movement struggling for a better world.

The other form of nonreligious fundamentalism offering a strong pull to disenchanted Evangelicals, especially men, is what Burton describes as "a modern atavism" that "promotes a nostalgic, masculinist vision of animal humanity." The dominant narrative of this network of believers goes something like this: "Once upon a time, . . . in a vanished age of gods and heroes, men were men and women were women. Human beings acted in accordance with their biological identity. Men fought wars. Women had babies." This movement laments the loss of traditional culture with its established norms and expected behaviors. Its followers believe that freedom has morphed into a feminized world of chaos. "They find spiritual and moral meaning," Burton says, "in primal, masculine (and at times *white*, primal, and masculine) images of heroic warriors of ages past."[40]

These new atavists reject the idea of identity being culturally conditioned. They believe nature itself determines identity. On the side of the movement that identifies as Christian, believers see themselves in a cosmic battle between good and evil. They are called to restore order—an order that puts everyone back in their natural, God-ordained place. Increasingly, they seem to believe that violence may be necessary to restore Christian America.

According to Charles Taylor, "Many believers (the fanatics, but also more than these) rest in the certainty that they have got God right (as against all those heretics and pagans in outer darkness). They are clutching on to an idol, to use a term familiar in the traditions of the God of Abraham." Such religion can be dangerous because "opening to transcendence is fraught with peril. But this is especially so if we respond to these perils by premature closure, drawing an

40. Burton, *Strange Rites*, 204–5.

unambiguous boundary between the pure and the impure through the polarization of conflict, even war."[41]

A segment of this movement finds meaning apart from religion. Their ideology is based on a "Darwinian brutality of nature," one that needs to be contended with, either by expressing it in violence or by ordering it in the structures of civilization. Competition is vital and necessary, whether it is physical, economic, or social. Groups such as the Proud Boys embody this ideology, and icons of this movement range from Canadian media personality and clinical psychologist Jordan Peterson to Donald Trump. For the most nihilistic of this group, those who see destruction of the establishment and apocalypse of judgment as the ultimate alternative, Alek Minassian, the perpetrator of the 2018 Toronto van attacks, serves as the icon.[42]

In an enchanted world, both good and evil exist. These powers interact with humans on a daily basis. They offer opportunities for the flourishing of life or the possibility of death. The ancient Christian catechetical document, the Didache, refers to these powers as "The Two Ways—the Way of Life or the Way of Death." Baptismal formulas in the second and third centuries included opportunities for believers to renounce the powers of darkness and to be sealed against those powers.

In their longing for enchantment, people are finding temporary solace and identity in what Burton describes as "strange rites" and in "the remixing of religious symbols." Some are closed off to the possibility of transcendent powers. Others are open to them. Whether they are open or closed to transcendence, many people in their hunger and searching will find themselves captive to destructive tendencies. They may be enticed by profane forms of antinomianism or by dangerous versions of nationalism.

The modern Bible seems to be powerless to keep today's religious seekers from falling under the spell of such dangers. In these strange and perilous days, we need an enchanted Bible, one with the ability to take us into a life-giving world, the world of God. People are hungry

41. Taylor, *Secular Age*, 769.
42. See Burton, *Strange Rites*, 201–37.

to go beyond the text and enter a world. *Sleep No More* offers a way to create the world of *Macbeth*, but this world is temporary, without eschatological hope. In the end it leaves participants empty and asking, "Is that all there is?" We need a Bible that opens for us a world of real presence, one that can shed the light of amazing grace and open before us the path that leads to the Way of Life. In order to provide these things, we have a large re-enchantment project ahead of us. It will involve constructing a new Christian social imaginary—namely, the way ordinary Christians see their social surroundings and express them in images and stories.[43]

This new Christian social imaginary will involve moving away from the current obsession with hermeneutics and into a deeper level of metaphysics and ontology. We need a new Christian imaginary where words such as *sacred*, *ethos*, and *cosmos* inhabit our discourse. An enchanted Christian social imaginary will involve revisiting what it means to be human and the nature of the divine-human relationship. In particular, the role the Bible plays in that relationship should look very different from the current one.

The land of Christian enchantment beckons to us. It is a land where, by the power of the Holy Spirit, Jesus continues to save, heal, and deliver. It is a land where, unlike the festival of Burning Man, the fires of the enchanting Festival of Pentecost are never extinguished. And it is a land where the Bible, by the power of the Holy Spirit, opens a portal into the mysterious realm of the life of God.

43. Taylor, *Secular Age*, 171–72.

4

The Contours of Enchantment

It is often easier to describe the features of disenchantment than to describe the contours of an enchanted world. This is because we can't quite put our finger on all that we've lost. However, in the many attempts to re-enchant the world, one can find some common threads: a longing for harmony and deep relationships; a longing for a unified cosmology, in which everything is connected; a world where the imagination is allowed to flourish and where play is welcomed; and a sense of otherness—something transcendent and grander than the immanent frame of our modern world.

A Harmonious World

The word *enchantment* comes from the Latin verb *cantare* (to sing) preceded by the preposition *in-* (into): *incantare*. This combination became the Old French *enchanter*, which passed into Middle English. At its root, enchantment means the experience of "finding oneself in a song" or "to sing into." An enchanted world is one in which there is harmony.

The ancient Greeks saw music as an expression of the order of the cosmos. Pythagoras is credited with discovering the deep order of music. As Robert Riley notes, "The significance that Pythagoras attributed to this discovery cannot be overestimated. Pythagoras thought that number was the key to the universe. When he found that harmonic music is expressed in exact numerical ratios of whole numbers, he concluded that music was the ordering principle of the world." For Pythagoras, "the harmonious sounds" made by humans, "either with their instruments or in their singing, were an approximation of a larger harmony that existed in the universe, also expressed by numbers, which was 'the music of the spheres.'"[1]

Writes Hans Boersma, "Early third-century theologian Clement of Alexandria (ca. 150–ca. 215) is particularly instructive here."[2] Boersma acknowledges that Clement's view of music "fit squarely within the Platonic approach that linked cosmic harmony, the harmony of the soul, and the harmony of music."[3] However, in Clement's *Exhortation to the Greeks*, "He refers to the eternal Word as the author of the cosmic harmony: 'He who sprang from David and yet was before him, the Word of God, scorned those lifeless instruments of lyre and harp. By the power of the Holy Spirit, He arranged in harmonious order this great world, yes, and the little world of man too, body and soul together; and on this many-voiced instrument of the universe He makes music to God, and sings to the human instrument.'" Boersma points out that Clement built upon the Platonic understanding of the cosmos existing as the harmony of *musica mundane*, even as he diverged from it. For Clement, "The Word of God introduces something altogether new; he is the 'New Song.'"[4]

In the twelfth century, Hildegard of Bingen, a mystic and doctor of the church, offered an enchanted vision of creation. The idea of cosmic harmony (*musica mundane*) was central to this vision. Hil-

1. Robert R. Riley, "The Music of the Spheres, or the Metaphysics of Music," Future Symphony Institute, https://www.futuresymphony.org/the-music-of-the-spheres-or-the-metaphysics-of-music/.

2. Hans Boersma, *Scripture as Real Presence: Sacramental Exegesis in the Early Church* (Grand Rapids: Baker Academic, 2017), 140.

3. Boersma, *Scripture as Real Presence*, 139.

4. Boersma, *Scripture as Real Presence*, 140.

degard understood that each of the elements possessed a "pristine sound that it had at the time of creation. . . . Fire has flames and sings in praise of God. Wind whistles a hymn to God as it fans and flames. And the human voice consists of words to sing paeans of praise. All creation is a single hymn in praise of God."[5]

For Hildegard, this harmony was tainted by the fall. "While he was still innocent, before his transgression, Adam's voice once beautifully blended with the voices of the angels in their praise of God. Adam lost his angelic voice and the Devil worked to 'eradicate the sweet beauty of spiritual hymns from the human heart.'"[6] Harmony was restored in Jesus Christ and continued in his church. For just as Jesus Christ was born of Virgin Mary through the Holy Spirit, so too the canticle of praise was rooted in the church through the Holy Spirit, "reflecting celestial harmony" (*symphonialis est anima*).[7]

It seems that J. R. R. Tolkien had in mind the ancient idea of the connection between music and the harmony of the cosmos when he penned the creation myth in *The Silmarillion*, the grand metanarrative that provides the background for *The Lord of the Rings*. In this account, music is what births creation. The music began in the mind of Eru (Ilúvatar), the One who shared with the Ainur, the Holy Ones, his singular mighty theme. As they discerned the music of the Creator, the Ainur sang the original "Great Music." This music consisted of "endless interchanging melodies woven in harmony that passed beyond hearing into the depths and into the heights, and the places of the dwelling of Ilúvatar were filled to overflowing, and the music and the echo of the music went out into the Void, and it was not void."[8]

The harmony in the Great Music did not last. It was interrupted by the discordant sounds of Melkor, one of the most powerful among

5. Hildegard of Bingen, *Analecta Sacra*, vol. 8, ed. J. B. Pitra (Monte Cassino, 1882), 352, as quoted in Heinrich Schipperges, *Hildegard of Bingen: Healing and the Nature of the Cosmos*, trans. John A. Broadwin (Princeton: Markus Wiener, 1998), 27.

6. *S. Hildegardis Abbatissae Opera*, ed. J. P. Migne, *Patrologia Latina* (Paris, 1856), 197:218–43; quoted by Schipperges, *Hildegard of Bingen*, 26.

7. Schipperges, *Hildegard of Bingen*, 26–27.

8. J. R. R. Tolkien, *The Silmarillion* (New York: Ballentine, 1979), 4.

the Ainur. He was a loner who would often go by himself into the void, hoping to find the power of the Flame Imperishable, the power that belonged alone to Ilúvatar. Melkor's music was his own; he strove not to harmonize but to compete. Many of the Ainur "who sang nigh him grew despondent, and their thought was disturbed and their music faltered; but some began to attune their music to his rather than to the thought which they had at first. Then the discord of Melkor spread ever wider, and the melodies which had been heard before foundered in a sea of turbulent sound."[9]

God's response to Job may also have served as the backdrop for Tolkien's creation story:

> Where were you when I laid the foundation of the earth?
> Tell me, if you have understanding.
>
> . . . when the morning stars sang together
> and all the heavenly beings shouted for joy?
>
> (Job 38:4, 7)

William Brown points out that "ancient Near Eastern cosmologies presumed a seamless connection between cosmos and society. Without categorical distinction, nature and civilization, cosmos and community, were the inseparable products of divinely instituted creation."[10] Up to the rise of the Enlightenment, most people inhabited an ethos reflecting cosmic unity. Ancient cosmologists developed designs for human community based on their own vision of the grand unity of things. Plato had his ideas, as did Aristotle. The Bible reveals a vision of a unified cosmology with God as the Creator.

Richard Rohr references the medieval concept of the "Great Chain of Being" as a metaphor for a unified ecology. "This was the philosophical/theological attempt to speak of the circle of life, the interconnectedness of all things on the level of pure 'Being.' If God is Being

9. Tolkien, *Silmarillion*, 4.

10. William P. Brown, *The Ethos of the Cosmos: The Genesis of Moral Imagination in the Bible* (Grand Rapids: Eerdmans, 1999), 3.

Itself (*Deus est Ens*), then the 'Great Chain' became a way of teaching and preserving the inherent dignity of all things that participate in that Divine Being in various ways."[11]

Rohr relates the Great Chain of Being to the biblical image of fullness, or pleroma (Gen. 2:1; Eph. 1:23). "Such a graphic metaphor held all things together in an enchanted universe. To stop recognizing the 'imago and similitudo' (Genesis 1:26) in any one link of the chain was to allow the entire coherence to fall apart! It would soon become a disenchanted universe. If we could not see the sacred in nature and creatures, we soon could not see it in ourselves, and finally we would not be able to see it at all (modern atheism)."[12] The Enlightenment and the rise of Cartesian philosophy, combined with Newtonian physics, created a rift in the vision of the organic unity of the cosmos.

Over the course of time, mind and matter continued to split, "driving a deep wedge between nature and humanity to the point of separating them out as 'self-contained realms.'"[13] Inhabiting the world in harmony gave way to perceiving and mastering the world. At the present time, we not only have the loss of an organic and unified cosmos but we also live in a world of competing perceptions; the discordant music of Melkor is normative. As seen at Burning Man, everyone is compelled to write their own music and construct their own ethos-habitation. These dwellings are fragile, temporary, and can easily be torn down for another updated version of reality.

A Relational World

Enchantment is deeply relational. One of the side effects of secularism is its ability to disrupt the relational cord that weaves the world and slice it into separate entities we call subjects and objects.

11. Richard Rohr, "A New Cosmology: Nature as the First Bible," Center for Action and Contemplation, http://cac.org/wp-content/uploads/2016/01/NatureastheFirstBible_digital-Insert.pdf.

12. Rohr, "New Cosmology."

13. Stephen Toulmin, *Cosmopolis: The Hidden Agenda of Modernity* (New York: Free Press, 1990), 67–69, as quoted in Brown, *Ethos of the Cosmos*, 13.

In this late age of modernity or the dawn of postmodernity, we all seem to be subjects, masters of our own fragile, objective worlds. A subject-object world is a disenchanted habitat, one that rips apart the seamless garment of life and creates a competitive wasteland where winners take all. It offers flourishing for some individuals with little concern for the common good.

In his "Letter from Birmingham Jail" Martin Luther King Jr. wrote, "In a real sense all life is inter-related. All men are caught in an inescapable network of mutuality, tied in a single garment of destiny. Whatever affects one directly, affects all indirectly. I can never be what I ought to be until you are what you ought to be, and you can never be what you ought to be until I am what I ought to be. . . . This is the inter-related structure of reality."[14]

A disenchanted world is one in which there is little common ground. Parker Palmer points out that "the root of the word 'reality' is the Latin *res*, meaning a property, a possession, a thing—a meaning most clearly seen in our terms 'real estate.'" Owning real estate is a means of gaining power. "Power comes from what we own and control, so the knowledge we value is that which gives us mastery over property."[15] In a disenchanted world, the Bible is part of the real estate, an object that can be bought and sold. As real estate, it is often used as a means of gaining power over the world rather than a space of the grace-filled land given to us.

God's revelation is always relational. In revelation, God is not so much giving us a deed to real estate as God is inviting us into his life. Revelation is God's personal "I AM," and Truth expressing the "I AM" is a mysterious relational web. There's no part of God's creation that exists in isolation. There's no part of God's revelation in Scripture that sits alone. Eugene Peterson observes, "Every part of the revelation, every aspect, every form is *personal*—God is relational to

14. Martin Luther King Jr., "Letter from Birmingham Jail" (April 16, 1963), Bill of Rights Institute, https://billofrightsinstitute.org/primary-sources/letter-from-birmingham-jail/.

15. Parker Palmer, *To Know as We Are Known: A Spirituality for Education* (New York: HarperCollins, 1983), 24.

the core—and so whatever is said, whatever is revealed, whatever is received is also personal and relational."[16]

In what is known as the "Final Discourse Sayings" (John 14–17), Jesus offers a description of the disciples' lives following his departure and the sending of the Holy Spirit. This description offers a glimpse into not only a relational Christianity but also a relational cosmos, one in which the life of God joins with humanity. Five sayings (14:16–17, 25–26; 15:26–27; 16:7–11, 12–15) together form a coherent unit on the nature of the divine-human relationship that would come about as a result of the Holy Spirit being sent.

1. The coming of the Spirit would bring experiential knowledge of God (14:7, 20) and would actualize the indwelling of the Father and Son, thus fulfilling the prayer of Christ for the unity of the disciples and their unity with the Godhead (17:21).
2. The Spirit would communicate the words of Jesus. The Paraclete would teach the disciples all things and remind them of everything he had said (14:25–26). In other words, the Spirit would make present Jesus's teachings. They would not be just a historical artifact but would be present in a living manner.
3. The Spirit would serve as an internal guide for the standards of the relational life in Christ. Love is to be the essential characteristic of this life. It is to be expressed in obedience to Jesus (14:15, 21, 23; 15:14). Loving obedience is also a means of communion with the Father (14:21, 23; 16:27), as well as characteristic of the relationship between the disciples (13:34; 15:9, 10, 12, 17).[17]

A key aspect of a holy enchantment is the relational thread between humanity and the natural world. Genesis 1 gives us a glimpse of the organic unity that Adam and Eve shared with their Edenic

16. Eugene Peterson, *Eat This Book: A Conversation in the Art of Spiritual Reading* (Grand Rapids: Eerdmans, 2006), 27.

17. Adapted from Jackie David Johns and Cheryl Bridges Johns, "Yielding to the Spirit: A Pentecostal Approach to Group Bible Study," *Journal of Pentecostal Theology* 1 (1992): 109–34.

coinhabitants. God saw everything he had created—the earth, its plants and animals, and humans—and saw that it was good. In Genesis 2 we see how God participated in this harmony. He invited Adam to name the animals, and he created Eve as partner to Adam. In Genesis 3 we see a picture of God as walking in the garden during the evening breeze. In the coming of sin, this unified ecology was broken.

There is a relational thread running through all creation—from its inception in the life of God to the eschaton. "All things are called into being out of God's living breath, and that breath 'holds them together' in a community of creation which furthers life," writes Jürgen Moltmann.[18] The relational thread has been marred and disenchanted, but it will be made new and complete. It is our eternal home, for which all creation groans.

> See, the home of God is among mortals.
> He will dwell with them as their God;
> they will be his peoples,
> and God himself will be with them.
>
> (Rev. 21:3)

Unified Cosmology

Enchantment means being part of a unified cosmology. Christians living in the era of science have a hard time defining the relationship between the so-called natural world and the supernatural. That is because a divorce between the two took place ages ago, one instigated not only by the Enlightenment's gradual closing off of the natural world from the supernatural but also by the Hellenistic influence on Western Christianity.

The influence of Neoplatonism, especially with theologians such as Origen and Augustine, helped create a dualism that continues today. For Origen, "The invisible and incorporeal things in heaven are true,

18. Jürgen Moltmann, *The Source of Life: The Holy Spirit and the Theology of Life*, trans. Margaret Kohl (London: SCM, 1997), 24.

but the visible and corporeal things on earth are copies of true things, not true in themselves."[19] Writes Thomas F. Torrance, "The implications of that dualist way of thinking were very far-reaching."[20] If things on the earth are not real in themselves, then the material world is of a lesser sacred value. If the material world is of a lesser sacred value, then it can be ignored, controlled, and even abused. Furthermore, salvation thus becomes a way of getting out of that lesser world into a nonmaterial "better world" (heaven).

In their book *Salvation Means Creation Healed*, Howard Snyder and Joel Scandrett write,

> How easy it is, then, for Christians to assume the divorce of heaven and earth. Many of us have unconsciously accepted a worldview that inverts the direction of salvation. We think salvation means going up to heaven rather than heaven coming to earth, as the Bible teaches. We have been taught that Jesus ascended to heaven so that our spirits could join him there eternally!—rather than what the Bible says: Jesus will come to earth to redeem all creation, including our own physical bodies. To a surprising degree, contemporary Christians are modern-day Gnostics.[21]

Patrick Curry points out that the only "legitimate" place these days to find the enchanted world of our ancestors, one that was both animate and sensuous, is in enchanted stories, such as Tolkien's *The Hobbit* and *The Lord of the Rings*. Curry observes that these stories grant us temporary access into a unified world where the lines between humans, other creatures, the earth's trees, and vegetation are quite thin. Tolkien's Middle Earth is not a passive objective background to the drama. "Far from it," writes Curry. "Middle Earth is an actor, a character itself, as are all the important pieces and parts." Curry highlights the

19. Origen, *In Canticum canticorum* [*Commentary on the Song of Songs*] 2.190, as quoted in Thomas F. Torrance, *Trinitarian Faith: The Evangelical Theology of the Ancient Catholic Church* (London: T&T Clark, 2004), 34–35.

20. Torrance, *Trinitarian Faith*, 34–35.

21. Howard A. Snyder with Joel Scandrett, *Salvation Means Creation Healed: The Ecology of Sin and Grace* (Eugene, OR: Cascade Books, 2011), 61.

importance of trees in Tolkien's writings. "In all my works, I take the part of trees against all of their enemies," wrote Tolkien in a letter. He once described *Lord of the Rings* as "my own internal Tree."[22]

Trees play an important part in the sacred cosmology of the Bible. Consider the creation account of Genesis 2: "Out of the ground the LORD God made to grow every tree that is pleasant to the sight and good for food" (v. 9). Two enchanting trees, the tree of life and the tree of the knowledge of good and evil, also grew in the garden. One tree held the power of opening human eyes to the reality of good and evil; eating the fruit of that tree brought the curse of death. The tree of life offered the possibility of living forever. When Adam and Eve were expelled from the garden, God placed "cherubim and a sword flaming and turning to guard the way to the tree of life" (3:24). The tree of life reappears in Revelation 22, the wondrous account of restored creation: "On either side of the river is the tree of life with its twelve kinds of fruit, producing its fruit each month; and the leaves of the tree are for the healing of the nations" (v. 2). Between these two bookends, trees play a prominent role in the Bible.[23]

C. S. Lewis sought to rescue Christianity from the evil enchantment of secularism, but he fell short of bringing the natural world and the spiritual world together into a more holistic, sacramental vision. For Lewis, the natural world is "the image, the symbol, that will pass away." Furthermore, "we are summoned to pass in through Nature, beyond her, into that splendour which she fitfully reflects."[24] Lewis's vision of the natural world reflects a Neoplatonic, Augustinian concept of the natural world as a sign that points to the Creator. For Lewis, God is seen *through* the beauty of creation, but it is dangerous to assume that there is real presence of God *in* nature itself. Worship of nature, the sign, could result in this lack of distinction. In other words, enchantment has its limits.

22. Patrick Curry, "Tolkien and Nature," Tolkien: The Official Site of the Tolkien Estate, https://www.tolkienestate.com/writing/patrick-curry-tolkien-and-nature/.

23. See Matthew Sleeth, *Reforesting Faith: What Trees Teach Us about the Nature of God and His Love for Us* (New York: WaterBrook, 2019).

24. C. S. Lewis, *The Weight of Glory* (San Francisco: HarperCollins, 2001), 42.

In his attempt to re-enchant the natural world, Alister McGrath maintains the same vision of the natural world that Lewis held. McGrath uses the analogy of Ulrich Zwingli's concept of the Eucharist as a symbolic reminder of a foundational event of the Christian faith. For Zwingli, the elements of the Eucharist do not become the body and blood of Christ, but meaning is given by the interpretation of those present. Likewise, McGrath understands "nature as a pointer to the glory of God, without requiring any change in the material reality of nature."[25]

McGrath's view of the natural world as "God's richly signed creation" leaves little space for a pneumatic cosmos. At best, creation serves as a foreshadowing of the new creation and as an "intimater of transcendence, hinting at a world beyond our experience."[26] McGrath's vision of the creation is devoid of an active, ongoing presence of the Spirit in the natural world. In fact, his book on re-enchanting nature has no reference to the Holy Spirit.

Paul Tillich identifies "the symbolic-romantic interpretation of nature" as "attempts to give back to nature its qualitative character" as well as its depth. However, Tillich says, "This view is very little aware of the real structure of nature" and substitutes pan-symbolism for pan-sacramentalism.[27] When nature is viewed as a symbol of the sacramental rather than a means of real presence, it is stripped of its organic relationship with the sacred; it remains disenchanted.

Writes Tillich, "The Protestant protest has rightly destroyed the magical elements in Catholic sacramentalism but has wrongly brought to the verge of disappearance the sacramental foundation of Christianity and with it the religious foundation of the protest itself." A rational, technical approach to nature emerged, and "the technical necessities somehow always assert themselves and create certain areas in which rational objectivity prevails. When this occurs, generally the magical view of nature disappears and is replaced by

25. Alister McGrath, *The Reenchantment of Nature: The Denial of Religion and the Ecological Crisis* (New York: Doubleday, 2002), 140.

26. McGrath, *Reenchantment of Nature*, 185.

27. Paul Tillich, *The Protestant Era*, trans. James Luther Adams (Chicago: University of Chicago Press, 1948), 101.

the rational-objective." According to Tillich, the technical control of nature causes it to be "objectified, and stripped of its qualities. No sacramental conception can find a root in this soil."[28]

Tillich's solution to Protestantism's disenchantment of Christianity is "an interpretation of nature which takes into account the intrinsic powers of nature." He suggests that "nature must be brought into the unity of the history of salvation."[29] In the first quarter of the twenty-first century, joining salvation history with creation continues to be a pressing issue in many forms of Protestantism.

The Two Books

The tradition of the two books—the Bible and creation—is rooted in a vision of a unified cosmology. This line of thinking understands both nature and Scripture as expressions of divine revelation; both are enchanted domains of God's presence. Augustine imaged creation as a divinely authored book: "Others, in order to find God, will read a book. Well, as a matter of fact, there is a certain great big book, the book of created nature. Look carefully at it top and bottom, observe it, read it. God did not make letters of ink for you to recognize him in; he set before your eyes all things he has made. Why look for a louder voice? Heaven and earth cries out to you, 'God made me.'"[30]

Writing within the framework of a Neoplatonic vision of the cosmos, Augustine believed that the natural world pointed to invisible things of the spiritual world. As a result, interpretation of nature was symbolic and multileveled, matching the same form of interpreting Scripture. William Wright and Francis Martin trace how the metaphysics of the two books shows up in the writings of the Greek fathers, St. Bonaventure, and John Calvin. They also point out that Calvin

28. Tillich, *Protestant Era*, 100.

29. Tillich, *Protestant Era*, 112.

30. Augustine, *Sermon* 68.6, in *Sermons 51–94*, trans. Edmund Hill, OP, *Works of Saint Augustine* 3/3 (Hyde Park, NY: New City, 1991), 225–26, as quoted in William M. Wright IV and Francis Martin, *Encountering the Living God in Scripture: Theological and Philosophical Principles for Interpretation* (Grand Rapids: Baker Academic, 2019), 110.

"likens creation to a book, which an individual with weak eyes can read only with the assistance of glasses (i.e., Scripture)."[31]

The two-books tradition can be seen in Galileo's 1615 "Letter to the Grand Duchess Christina," in which he wrote, "The holy Bible and the phenomena of nature proceed alike from the divine Word."[32] Later Enlightenment thinkers collapsed the Bible into the natural world, leaving only one book as a legitimate means of knowledge. Baruch Spinoza argued that the "Bible should be studied according to the way in which people study the natural world."[33] He makes this point because "he regards God and nature as identical," say Wright and Martin.[34] Spinoza's denial of transcendence made a way for the synergy between the natural and the supernatural worlds to collapse.

The demise of the two-books tradition and the disappearance of the transcendent leads conservative Christians to respond in one of two ways: either they choose to ignore the natural world in favor of the Bible as the "one book," or they try to use the Bible as a scientific text to explain the natural world. In both instances, there is a great gulf between the transcendent and immanent realms. In the former, the transcendent is locked away in heaven, but the Bible gives us a record of it. In the latter, the Bible is consumed within the immanent frame of modernity and thus becomes a scientific text of sorts.

Pentecostalism's Opportunity

It is a strange irony that many Pentecostals fall short in seeing how much the natural world is embedded with the glory of the

31. Wright and Martin, *Encountering the Living God*, 111. See John Calvin, *Institutes of the Christian Religion*, ed. John T. McNeill, trans. Ford Lewis Battles, Library of Christian Classics (Philadelphia: Westminster, 1961), 1:51–66.

32. Galileo Galilei, "Letter to the Grand Duchess Christina," in *Discoveries and Opinions of Galileo*, trans. Stillman Drake (Garden City, NY: Doubleday, 1957), 186, quoted in Wright and Martin, *Encountering the Living God*, 112.

33. Baruch Spinoza, *Theologico-Political Treatise,* trans. R. H. M. Elwes (New York: Dove, 1959), 99, as quoted in Wright and Martin, *Encountering the Living God*, 149.

34. Wright and Martin, *Encountering the Living God*, 149.

supernatural. Few in my tradition stop to reflect on the meaning of being Spirit-filled as the comingling of the material (the human body) and the spiritual. As heirs of the Enlightenment, most Pentecostals have bought into the idea that there is a great split between the material and the spiritual. Believing they need to make a choice between the two, they take the road of the spiritual and, in doing so, create a form of spirituality that is a poor representation of the great natural harvest festival: Pentecost.

In recent years, an increasing number of Pentecostal/Charismatic theologians have begun to better articulate the dynamics of their spirituality and how it bridges the gap between the material and the spiritual. In his article defining a Pentecostal worldview, Jackie Johns writes, "The Pentecostal worldview is God-centered. All things relate to God and God relates to all things. This fusion of God with the phenomenological does not collapse God into creation. Instead, it is a predisposition to see the transcendent God at work in, with, through, above, and beyond all."[35]

James K. A. Smith offers an explicit Pentecostal "social imaginary" in which exists a worldview containing the dynamics of enchanted theology of creation and culture. "Endemic to a Pentecostal worldview," he writes, "is the implicit affirmation of the dynamic, active presence of the Spirit not only in the church, but also in creation. And not only the Spirit, but also other spirits. Thus central to a Pentecostal construal of the world is a sense of 'enchantment.'"[36]

Smith's vision of a pneumatic cosmology is one in which nature is "suspended in the Spirit of creation" as well as "charged with the Spirit's presence."[37] Drawing from the "participatory ontology associated with the *nouvelle theologie*,"[38] as well as its contemporary

35. Jackie David Johns, "Pentecostalism and the Postmodern Worldview," *Journal of Pentecostal Theology* 7 (1995): 73–96.

36. James K. A. Smith, *Thinking in Tongues: Pentecostal Contributions to Christian Philosophy* (Grand Rapids: Eerdmans, 2010), 39.

37. Smith, *Thinking in Tongues*, 40.

38. See John Milbank, *The Suspended Middle: Henri de Lubac and the Debate concerning the Supernatural* (Grand Rapids: Eerdmans, 2005).

manifestation as "Radical Orthodoxy,"[39] Smith offers a "nondualistic supernaturalism," or a "supernatural materialism":

> On the one hand, it affirms that matter *as created* exceeds itself and *is* only insofar as it participates in or is suspended from the transcendent Creator; on the other hand, it affirms that there is a significant sense in which the transcendent inheres in immanence. "Things," then—and the created order in general—do not have . . . some kind of inalienable right to be. Rather, *being* is a gift from the transcendent Creator such that things exist only insofar as they participate in the being of the Creator—whose Being is Goodness.[40]

Amos Yong is another example of a Pentecostal theologian who stands as an exception to the tendency to bifurcate the natural and the spiritual dimensions. He has written prolifically on the intersections between science and faith and the interconnections of the natural with the pneumatic. Yong claims that "there is a genuine and systemic inter-relationality—between male and female; between human and other sentient beings; between sentient beings and the natural world; between the natural and spiritual domains, etc.—brought about by the Spirit."[41] In contrast to McGrath, Yong offers a "pneumatological understanding of the creation." He believes such a view is "poised to negotiate the tensions between the created order as systematically interrelated and interconnected on the one hand, and the created order as en-spirited, emergent, and dynamic on the other."[42]

Yong invites theologians to "think analogically about the relationship between theology, concerned with the book of Scripture, and contemporary science, concerned with the book of nature." He writes, "If the work of the Spirit was to harmonize the many tongues on

39. See James K. A. Smith, *Introducing Radical Orthodoxy: Mapping a Post-Secular Theology* (Grand Rapids: Baker Academic, 2012).

40. Smith, *Thinking in Tongues*, 100.

41. Amos Yong, "Toward a Pneumato-Ecological Ethic," in *An Amos Yong Reader*, ed. Christopher A. Stephenson (Eugene, OR: Cascade Books, 2020), 107.

42. Yong, "Toward a Pneumato-Ecological Ethic," 107.

the Day of Pentecost so as not to eliminate their differences but to declare the wonders of God (Acts 2:11), then might it not be possible for the same Spirit today to harmonize the many discursive practices of the various theological, natural, and human sciences so as not to eliminate their differences but to exalt the glory, power, and goodness of God?"[43] Ultimately, Yong calls for more dialogue between theology and science. He writes, "The church has long believed that God has revealed His glory in His two books: Scripture and nature. If the Holy Spirit leads the people of God into all truth, will not the Spirit lead theologians and scientists together also in unveiling the truth of God and the world?"[44]

Wolfgang Vondey offers a Pentecostal metaphysics in which the "doctrine of creation is subsumed under soteriology as an indication that the meaning of the universe is found not in the product or act of creation itself but in the redemption of the cosmos."[45] For Vondey, "Creation is the economy of salvation in a Pentecostal narrative that begins and ends with God, punctuated by the experiences and interaction of human beings with different powers in a 'spirit-filled' cosmos that engages perichoretically four broad spheres: (1) the divine, (2) the human, (3) the natural world, and (4) the realm of evil."[46]

The works of Smith, Yong, and Vondey represent a new era in Pentecostal theology. These theologians are daring to explore the meaning of being Spirit-filled as it relates to metaphysics, ontology, and epistemology. They offer a way beyond modernity's bifurcated discussions concerning the natural and the supernatural as well as a generative path forward. This generative path is one that all Christians, not just Pentecostals, will benefit from.

43. Amos Yong, "The Books of Scripture and of Nature," in Stephenson, *Amos Yong Reader*, 89.

44. Amos Yong, "Faith and Science," in Stephenson, *Amos Yong Reader*, 95.

45. Wolfgang Vondey, "Religion at Play: Pentecostalism and the Transformation of a Secular Age," *Pneuma* 40 (2018): 27. See also Vondey, *Pentecostal Theology: Living the Full Gospel* (New York: Bloomsbury, 2017), 155–74.

46. Vondey, "Religion at Play," 27.

Unfinished Business

When it comes to a vision of cosmic unity, Christians have a lot of unfinished business. The re-enchantment of Christianity depends on a renewed vision of cosmic unity. The world that began and continues to be sustained by the Spirit-Word is a beautiful and mysterious synergy between the so-called material and spiritual. It is a world that is robustly embodied, while at the same time containing dimensions that are unseen by human eyes. Gerard Manley Hopkins's poem "God's Grandeur" beautifully expresses the worn wonder of it all:

> The world is charged with the grandeur of God.
> It will flame out, like shining from shook foil;
> It gathers to a greatness, like the ooze of oil
> Crushed. Why do men then now not reck his rod?
> Generations have trod, have trod, have trod;
> And all is seared with trade; bleared, smeared with toil;
> And wears man's smudge and shares man's smell: the soil
> Is bare now, nor can foot feel, being shod.
>
> And for all this, nature is never spent;
> There lives the dearest freshness deep down things;
> And though the last lights off the black West went
> Oh, morning, at the brown brink eastward, springs—
> Because the Holy Ghost over the bent
> World broods with warm breast and with ah! bright wings.[47]

As a consequence of bad theology, which separates the material world from the spiritual, far too many Christians live with little attention to the "dearest freshness deep down things." Fearing accusations of pantheism or of being "New Age," they have constructed a social imaginary in which the natural world is devoid of any transcendent dimensions. At best, the transcendent can punch holes in

47. Gerard Manley Hopkins, "God's Grandeur," in *Poems and Prose*, ed. W. H. Gardner (New York: Penguin Classics, 1953), 27.

the immanent frame (an interventionist supernaturalism), but these holes are temporary: they quickly close.

Most modern Christians have learned to live with this divorce between heaven and earth. In fact, they've become quite comfortable with it. Like children of divorced parents, they get to live with one parent (the immanent frame of the natural world) and visit the other parent on Sundays (the transcendent, spiritual world). In the day-to-day reality, their social imaginary is operatively immanent. "We now inhabit this self-sufficient immanent order, *even if we believe in transcendence*," writes Smith.[48]

This imaginary, one in which the natural world is not infused with transcendence, makes it difficult for us to have a healthy relationship with the creation. At worst, we fall into the deadly trap of seeing it as a vast collection of resources. At best, we see the creation as an object that needs protection and care. The key in both instances is that the creation is seen as something outside of ourselves, something that we either use or care for.

Living in an immanently framed world, far too many Christians are infected with the malady Richard Louv identifies as "nature-deficit disorder."[49] Diminished senses, attention issues, and high rates of physical and mental illnesses characterize nature-deficit disorder. Nature-deficit disorder is closely related to enchantment-deficit disorder. Both disorders keep us from fully participating in the world. Both stunt our innate capacity to experience the wide range of sensuous life, one in which we see, hear, taste, and feel the revelation of God.

Within Western Christianity, where transcendence is largely framed out of ordinary life, there is no longer a sense of the "two books." There is only one book, the Bible. It has to do the heavy weightlifting of all things transcendent, especially in Protestant churches where the Eucharist is no longer enchanted. To make matters worse, the Bible can't do its heavy lifting because it too exists within an immanent

48. James K. A. Smith, *How (Not) to Be Secular: Reading Charles Taylor* (Grand Rapids: Eerdmans, 2014), 92.

49. Richard Louv, *The Last Child in the Woods: Saving Our Children from Nature-Deficit Disorder* (Chapel Hill, NC: Algonquin Books, 2005).

frame. People keep it around, but it may or may not be read. They sometimes bring it to church on Sunday mornings, but due to rising excarnation, it seems out of place. When reading the Bible in a disenchanted world, people may have a momentary sense of being in the presence of something grandly "Other," but such sensibility can be easily shut down in the immanent frame of modernity.

Flourishing of the Imagination

An enchanted world is one in which the imagination flourishes, where reason and imagination are joined together in creative harmony. Throughout history, the imagination has been elevated and then demoted as a means of knowing the world. In her thick account of the imagination, Jennifer Anna Gosetti-Ferencei writes, "Historically, imagination has been most persistently identified as the capacity for internal representation of perceptions retained in memory." She notes that for Plato, this definition of imagination was problematic because it meant that "imagination merely, and often inaccurately, copied sense perceptions, themselves at a remove from the essential truth of things that could be grasped only by reason." In this way, imagination "was thought to undermine knowledge."[50] For Aristotle, in contrast, the imagination offered the possibility of what *could* happen, and this made it productive.

Gosetti-Ferencei points out that "in the early modern philosophy of Michel de Montaigne, René Descartes, and Blaise Pascal, the imagination was demoted again to an inessential role, and a renewed anxiety arose about imagination's impact on thinking." She continues: "Rational thinking and productions of the fancy are assigned to distinct faculties, with the former alone considered essential. To confuse imagination and perception, cognition proper and fantasy, is to court illusion, error, and even madness."[51]

50. Jennifer Anna Gosetti-Ferencei, *The Life of Imagination: Revealing and Making the World* (New York: Columbia University Press, 2018), 6.

51. Gosetti-Ferencei, *Life of Imagination*, 6.

Later philosophers, such as Immanuel Kant, came to recognize imagination's close ties to other modes of thinking, Gosetti-Ferencei writes. Some things, such as "the perception of beauty and other aesthetic qualities," could not "be entirely captured by rational thought." The Romantics championed the cause of the imagination. Samuel Taylor Coleridge saw it "as the force of creativity." The German Romantics, such as Friedrich Schlegel, understood imagination as indirect access "to the unity of life itself."[52]

In spite of some previous rich discussions, during most of the twentieth century the discussions regarding imagination were more tempered; imagination took a back seat to the power of rational thought. Swiss psychologist Jean Piaget conducted research into cognitive development and mapped the imaginative ecology of early childhood. In particular, Piaget observed how play took a prominent role in developing a child's cognitive capacities. Piaget understood play to be the primary means of a child's knowing the world. Yet in mapping the higher stages of cognitive development, Piaget understood imagination and play as receding into the background in favor of abstract reasoning.[53]

Albert Einstein had no problem in joining the imagination with abstract reasoning. "Imagination is more important than knowledge," he said. "For knowledge is limited, whereas imagination embraces the entire world, stimulating progress, giving birth to evolution. It is, strictly speaking, a real factor in scientific research."[54]

C. S. Lewis provided his own critique of modernity's banishing of imagination. In *Prince Caspian*, Lewis describes the disenchantment of Narnia taking place during a time when the Telmarines rule there. The Telmarines are warriors and builders. They have no time for the magic of talking animals and enchanted forests. Prince Caspian, nephew to the Telmarine king, learns of the magic of the old days

52. Gosetti-Ferencei, *Life of Imagination*, 7.

53. See Jean Piaget and Barbel Inhelder, *The Psychology of the Child* (New York: Basic Books, 2000).

54. Albert Einstein, *On Cosmic Religion: With Other Opinions and Aphorisms* (Mineola, NY: Dover Publications, 2009), 49.

from his tutor. Not realizing he is treading on dangerous ground, the prince goes to his uncle to inquire about the time when Narnia was enchanted. He receives a stinging rebuke: "'That's all nonsense, for babies,' said the King sternly. . . . 'You're getting too old for that sort of stuff. At your age you ought to be thinking of battles and adventures, not fairy tales.'"[55]

A reason-based faith is one of the by-products of Protestant Christianity's attempt to deconstruct the magic of Roman Catholicism. Within Evangelicalism, this turn to reasoned faith further facilitated imagination's marginalization. For instance, the language of "making a decision for Christ" highlighted conversion as a matter of cognitive assent. Evangelistic methods such as "The Roman Road" involved getting a person to agree with logical deductive reasoning:

> Because of our sin, we are separated from God. (Rom. 3:23)
> The penalty for our sin is death. (Rom. 6:23)
> Jesus Christ paid the penalty for our sin. (Rom. 5:8)
> If we repent and believe in Jesus Christ, we are saved. (Rom. 10:13)

During the twentieth century, Evangelicals were heavily influenced by the developmental theories of Piaget and Lawrence Kolhberg. As a result, Sunday school classes were carefully age-graded according to a person's cognitive capacity. Young children were given opportunities for creative, imaginative play; but in the higher levels, true to form, these dynamics dropped off in favor of methods aimed at "understanding the faith." By the time a person progressed to adulthood, it was understood that they were primarily a cognitive, thinking being. Within the immanent frame of the Evangelical world, mystery, transcendence, and the imagination found little space wherein to flourish.

By the 1990s, young adults who had grown up in churches where there was little space for the imagination began to create their own, more enchanted forms of the faith. The Emergent Church movement arose as sort of a rebellion against the long-suppressed imagination.

55. C. S. Lewis, *Prince Caspian* (1951; repr. New York: Harper Collins, 2007), 43.

Members of this movement attempted to embody their faith. They revived ancient practices such as prayer labyrinths, chants, *lectio divina*, anointing with oil, and weekly Eucharist. Emergents imaginatively played in the design of worship spaces, bringing back incense, candles, crosses, and icons. The sensibility of the Emergents continues in various forms of Evangelical Christianity. The rise of Anglican spirituality is but one example.

Within the world at large, we are seeing a renaissance of the imagination. It is becoming the focus of study in various disciplines: the humanities, neuroscience, cognitive and developmental psychology, and anthropology, to name a few. Theologians and biblical scholars are bringing the imagination back into their discussions. Amos Yong's work in the pneumatological imagination represents a creative attempt to plumb the depths of the intersection between creativity, the imagination, and the Spirit.

A renewed emphasis on the imagination is good news for those seeking to re-enchant the world. It is especially good news for those desiring to re-enchant Christianity. In the words of Janine Langan, "Imagination is our fundamental mode of insertion in the world, . . . therefore it has deep religious implications."[56] Eugene Peterson sees the imagination as "one of the essential ministries in nurturing the life of faith. For faith is not a leap out of the everyday but a plunge into its depths."[57]

Imagination enables us to think beyond the present. It is not an escape from the world. Rather, it is the capacity to make the world, to transform the common into the extraordinary. Creativity and imagination go hand in hand. There can be no creativity without imagination and no imagination without creativity. Enchantment involves both imagination and creativity.

The narrative structure of stories has a particular power to facilitate imagination. Myths and stories pull us away from the mundane

56. Janine Langan, "The Christian Imagination," in *The Christian Imagination*, ed. Leland Ryken (New York: WaterBrook Press, 2002), 64.

57. Eugene Peterson, *Run with the Horses: The Quest for Life at Its Best*, 2nd ed. (Downers Grove, IL: InterVarsity, 2009), 74.

and transport us into other worlds. They also help us make sense of our world. The field of narrative psychology investigates the power of stories in making sense of the world. This field is based on the assumption that a person's life is a story, a plot filled with protagonists, antagonists, and all sorts of other characters. One's life is a tale, weaving together the good and the bad, great tragedy as well as times of joy. Far too often, deep pathos haunts the stories of human existence.

Tolkien understood fairy stories as having the power of what he called *eucatastrophe*. Unlike the tragedy form of classical drama, *eucatastrophe* is the "good catastrophe, the sudden joyous 'turn' . . . [that] is not essentially 'escapist' or 'fugitive.' In its fairy-tale—or otherworld—setting it is a sudden and miraculous grace: never to be counted on to recur." It does not "deny the existence of *dyscatastrophe*, of sorrow and failure, the possibility of these is necessary to the joy of delieverance. It denies . . . universal final defeat, and in so far is *evangelium*, giving a fleeting glimpse of Joy, Joy beyond the walls of the world, poignant as grief."[58]

Tolkien believed in approaching the Christian story as a form of *eucatastrophe*, God redeeming corrupt humankind. In this sense, he understood the Gospels as "embracing all the essence of fairy-stories." For Tolkien, "The birth of Christ is *the eucatastrophe* of [human] history. The Resurrection is *the eucatastrophe* of the Incarnation. The story begins and ends in joy."[59] To Tolkien's narrative, I would add that Pentecost is the *Grand Eucatastrophe*, the Great High Feast that celebrates the outpouring of joy on all creation.

The Centrifugal Power of Otherness

An enchanted world is charged with otherness, a sense that someone or something beyond us has power over us. "In the enchanted world,"

58. J. R. R. Tolkien, "On Fairy Stories," in *Essays Presented to Charles Williams* (Oxford: Oxford University Press, 1947), as quoted in Ryken, *Christian Imagination*, 365.

59. Tolkien, "Fairy Stories," as quoted in Ryken, *Christian Imagination*, 366.

writes Charles Taylor, "the meaning exists already outside of us, prior to contact; it can take us over; we can fall into its field of force. It comes on us from the outside."[60]

The power of otherness conveys the centrifugal force that is able to pull people outside of their own sphere of life. Such power is not the same as the postmodern sense of radical otherness, in which the other's difference disrupts one's equilibrium. Enchantment does not merely happen in the human realm. There is a higher power at work. It shatters the atomistic view of the human subject and radically decenters it.

Taylor describes enchantment as "what we usually call 'magic' powers: blessed objects, e.g., relics of saints, the Host, candles, are full of God-power, and can do some of the good things which God's power does, like heal diseases and fight off disasters. Sources of evil power correspondingly wreak malevolent ends, make us sick, weaken our cattle, blight our crops, and the like."[61]

Such enchantment was the social imaginary that framed the writing of the Bible. For instance, Mark's Gospel describes a world in which the supernatural does not stay politely in the background. It impinges on the lives of people, such as the Gerasene man who was held captive by many demons (Mark 5:1–20). In all the Gospels, Jesus is portrayed as the only source of power to break the hold of evil. His miracles—feeding the multitudes, healing the sick, raising the dead, and setting the demon-possessed free—usher in a new age of the kingdom of God.

The power of otherness can take two forms: wonder and the possibility of deconstruction. Wonder is central to enchantment. It is an expansiveness that pulls us outward, beyond ourselves. Then also, it is a state of feeling possible. As Sharon Blackie writes, "Wonder allows us to break through the constraints, to reach beyond the restrictive cognitive frameworks we've been tethered to, so that we can entertain the possible rather than simply observing the actual."[62]

60. Charles Taylor, *A Secular Age* (Cambridge, MA: Harvard University Press, 2007), 34.

61. Taylor, *Secular Age*, 34–35.

62. Sharon Blackie, *The Enchanted Life: Unlocking the Magic of the Everyday* (Toronto: House of Anansi, 2018), 77.

William James believed that wonder was central to being human. One could not truly know the world without wonder. "It sees the familiar as if it were strange, and the strange as if it were familiar. It can take things up and lay them down again. Its mind is full of air that plays round every subject. It rouses us from our native dogmatic slumber and breaks up our caked prejudices."[63] In the words of Josef Pieper, "Wonder signifies that the world is profounder, more all-embracing and mysterious than the logic of everyday reason had taught us to believe."[64]

Unfortunately, we live in a wonder-deficient world. No longer open to the transcendent, people struggle to experience the mysterious pull of wonder. Wonder deficit is closely related to nature-deficit disorder. Nature has a way of inducing wonder: majestic sunsets, beautiful mountains, whales sporting in the ocean, the first flowers of spring, fall leaves shimmering like gold.

All too often we close ourselves in rooms where technology claims our attention. Technology has its own enchantment, but far too often its wonders have a centripetal force, pulling us inward, down rabbit holes of information. Technology has the power to shut down the parts of our brain that engage the imagination. In the worst sense, it can stupefy us, dulling our senses. With the current overreliance on passive technology, we've become good at sorting and labeling information. But capacities for creativity, wonder, and divergent thinking are being rapidly diminished. All of us seem to be in need of a sense of otherness with the power to pull us outward into a larger, transcendent realm.

The power of otherness goes beyond wonder into the realm of the dangerous. Great myths often contain beings with the power to give life as well as destroy it. In *The Simarillion*, Melkor pulled some of the Ainur into his discordant realm. Chief among them was Sauron, who became Melkor's chief lieutenant. Sauron established Melkor's reign in Middle Earth. Sauron's power drew some of the Elves. They were so marred by this power that their majestic beauty dissolved,

63. William James, *Some Problems of Philosophy: A Beginning of an Introduction to Philosophy* (Cambridge, MA: Harvard University Press, 1979), 11.

64. Josef Pieper, "The Philosophical Act," in *Leisure: The Basis of Culture* (San Francisco: Ignatius, 2009), 115.

and they became grotesque orcs. As Sauron's power of enchantment grew, it captured men, turning them against one another and forcing them to serve as allies in his destructive path. His power consumed everything in its path, turning the verdant beauty of Middle Earth into a wasteland. The power of good eventually won over Sauron's dark evil, but at a great cost.

In C. S. Lewis's *Chronicles of Narnia*, the great lion Aslan is the King above all High Kings in the land of Narnia. In a conversation between Susan, one of the humans who had come through the wardrobe into Narnia, and a talking beaver, Susan asks about Aslan: "'Is he—quite safe? I shall feel rather nervous about meeting a lion.' . . . 'Safe?' said Mr. Beaver . . . 'Who said anything about safe? 'Course he isn't safe. But he's good. He's the King, I tell you.'"[65] Aslan's power is so great that his presence invokes wonder, even as it instills fear. But the power of otherness represented in this character is power for the good. It is lifegiving.

In Scripture we can see Satan's otherness-power. It is the power to entice and destroy. We also see God's great otherness. God's goodness is such that his power is intent on restoring the creation, marred and broken in the fall. It is this goodness by which God sent the only begotten Son—Jesus Christ—to restore all broken creation and to destroy evil.

Within the immanent frame of modernity, we have lost much of the capacity to experience wonder. We are in need of an enchanted vision, one that gives us eyes to see the alluring yet destructive power of evil. Likewise, we need eyes to see the magnificent power of the Creator God and the wondrous, restoring goodness found in the incarnation of Jesus Christ.

65. C. S. Lewis, *The Lion, the Witch and the Wardrobe* (1950; repr. New York: Collier, 1970), 86.

5

Hopeful Signs

The current haunting-longing for enchantment is making its way into discussions about the Bible. I believe these discussions are hopeful signs that the cracks in modern Christianity's immanent frame are opening to let in more of the air of transcendence. During the past few years there have been some worthy attempts to re-enchant the biblical text. These attempts are noteworthy because they offer new ways of seeing the Bible apart from traditional modernist and postmodernist categories. They employ terms and images to describe the Bible that are, in many ways, premodern, bringing back words such as *holy* and *sacred*.

These theologians, biblical scholars, and pastors are seeking to rebaptize the text, returning it to the realm of the numinous and the mysterious. They are all attempting to define Scripture in ontological categories that go beyond the parameters of discussions about the meaning of inspiration or categories of foundationalism or postfoundationalism. They are worth noticing because their writings point toward transcendence, mystery, and the Bible's relationship with God's mission to restore and heal creation.

Among these somewhat disparate approaches to the biblical text are common themes of sacred and sacramental space, Scripture's mission in the economy of salvation, and the radical otherness of the biblical text. Each approach offers a sense of richness and depth that was lost during the Scripture wars of late modernity. In that sense, these approaches to the Bible take us out of the hermeneutical trench lines of late modernity and invite us to envision a Bible filled with sacred presence and deep mysteries.

The Bible as Thin Place

Peter Gomes represents a mainline Protestant attempt to re-enchant the text. In his work *The Good Book*, which became a *New York Times* bestseller, Gomes acknowledges the startlingly high rate of biblical illiteracy. But he also acknowledges that "many people want to do something about their biblical illiteracy. There is something there that they feel they ought to know about, and yet they are frustrated in their attempts to read the Bible and make sense of it themselves."[1]

In response to the rising problem of biblical illiteracy, Gomes seeks to reimagine the nature of the Bible. He offers a vision of the Bible as "dynamic, living, alive, lively." This means that "behind the letter of the text is the spirit that animates it, the force that gave it and gives it life." He continues: "There is something always elusive about the Bible. . . . The text actually adapts itself to our capacity to hear it. Thus we hear not as first-century Christians, nor even as eighteenth-century Christians, but as men and women alive here and now." Gomes sees the reading and hearing of Scripture as a Pentecostal experience in which "we hear them telling in our own tongues the mighty works of God."[2]

Gomes envisions the Holy Spirit as an active presence enlivening all the powers of good scholarship. Those powers "are merely means by which the living spirit of the text is taken from one context and appropriated totally into ours. . . . In this sense, then, Scripture is both transformed and transformative; that is to say, our understanding of what it says and means evolves, and so too do we as a result. This

1. Peter Gomes, *The Good Book: Reading the Bible with Mind and Heart* (San Francisco: Harper, 1996), 7.

2. Gomes, *Good Book*, 20.

transformation does not always repudiate what was before, but it does always transcend it."[3]

Gomes refers to the biblical text as creating a "thin place," similar to the thin places found in ancient Celtic spirituality. Scripture serves as a threshold place where two worlds meet. He reimages the Bible as "the place where not only others long dead but we ourselves encounter those thin places of suffering, joy, and mystery."[4]

As much as Gomes uses the language of thin places, he falls short of imaging the metaphysics of the biblical text. The Bible remains an artifact, "a record of holy encounters."[5] He approaches the Bible using a postfoundational hermeneutic, understanding the Bible as a "guide through the thin places, and as providing us with a record of how our ancestors coped with their encounters, and guidance beyond their particular situation which may be useful in ours."[6] These moves are helpful, but they fall short of re-enchanting the Bible.

In Gomes's vision of the text, nothing surrounds the metaphysical nature of the Bible that creates a space for the two worlds of the natural and supernatural to meet. Gomes continues to operate out of the immanent frame of modernity, while inching toward another form of metaphysics. For Gomes, reading the Bible "with fear and trembling" is necessary. Yet there is no sense of *radical otherness* that would create a need for fear and trembling.

The Bible as Sacrament

The Protestant Reformers, in their zeal to dispel magic from the church's rituals, and in their championing of *sola scriptura*, helped move Protestantism out of its premodern sacred cosmos into the rational "scientific" world emerging at that time. The result was a Bible lacking in sacramental status and not having the power to mediate divine presence.

3. Gomes, *Good Book*, 21.
4. Gomes, *Good Book*, 216.
5. Gomes, *Good Book*, 34.
6. Gomes, *Good Book*, 215.

Writing in the mid-twentieth century, Tillich notes that the issue of the sacramental was one that Protestantism had not adequately addressed. He calls for Protestants to "deal seriously with the whole sacramental aspect of religion."[7] Tillich saw how the Reformers had left little in terms of a sacred ethos, an ethos necessary for religion to flourish. He observes, "The Protestant protest has rightly destroyed the magical elements in Catholic sacramentalism but has wrongly brought to the verge of disappearance the sacramental foundation of Christianity and with it the religious foundation of the protest itself."[8] For Tillich, it was important "to draw the line between the spiritual and the magical use of the sacramental element, for this element is the one essential element of every religion, namely, the presence of the divine before our acting and striving, in a 'structure of grace,' and in the symbols expressing it."[9]

During the early part of the twenty-first century, the sacramental element is finding its way back into the lives of Protestants. We can see this rise of the sacramental in people who are finding a home in ancient liturgies. We can also see the rise of the sacramental in discussions surrounding the nature of Scripture. Two theologians stand out for their efforts to reclaim the sacramental nature of the Bible: Marcus Borg and Hans Boersma. Although they represent two different Protestant traditions—mainline Protestantism and Anglicanism—they weave common threads into their sacramental tapestries.

Marcus Borg

Marcus Borg acknowledges that as "we enter the twenty-first century, we need a new set of lenses through which to read the Bible." He perceives that "the older set [of lenses], ground and polished by modernity, no longer works for millions of people."[10] Noting that

7. Paul Tillich, *The Protestant Era*, trans. James Luther Adams (Chicago: University of Chicago Press, 1948), 94.

8. Tillich, *Protestant Era*, xxii.

9. Tillich, *Protestant Era*, xxiii.

10. Marcus Borg, *Reading the Bible Again for the First Time: Taking the Bible Seriously but Not Literally* (San Francisco: HarperCollins, 2001), 3.

"conflict about how to see and read the Bible is the single greatest issue dividing Christians in North America today," Borg seeks to rescue the Bible from "fact fundamentalists." He makes the point that "both biblical fundamentalists and Christian liberals are often fact fundamentalists. For the former, the Bible must be factually true in order to be true. . . . They emphasize the literal and historical factuality of biblical texts."[11] For those in the latter group, the strategy is quite different. They are "seeking to rescue a few facts from the fire."[12] The Jesus Seminar is a good example of the liberal quest to save what can still be saved.[13]

Attempting to avoid both forms of modern reductionism, Borg envisions the biblical text as a sacrament of the sacred; it occasions the experience of God. Borg illustrates such sacramental moments in the practice of *lectio divina*, the contemplative reading of the text a number of times, with periods of silence between each reading. The purpose of *lectio divina* is to "listen for the Spirit of God speaking through words of the biblical text."[14]

What is evident in Borg's writings is a sincere desire to re-enchant the biblical text. Like Gomes, he attempts to point in the direction of mystery and wonder. He offers a pneumatological reading of the Bible, one in which the Holy Spirit is present in the reading. However, as with Gomes, Borg moves into postfoundationalist grounds, viewing the Bible as a human document that came out of and in return shapes the cultural-linguistic world of Christianity.

Borg advocates reading the Bible as a combination of history—the tool of historical criticism—and metaphor. Utilizing a postliberal

11. Borg, *Reading the Bible Again*, 16.

12. Borg, *Reading the Bible Again*, 32.

13. Robert Funk began the Jesus Seminar in 1985. Comprised of both scholars and laypersons, its purpose was to locate "the historical Jesus." Members of the group used various historical-critical methods to determine the historicity of the words and deeds of Jesus. In 2006, the group turned their focus to the development of the Jesus tradition in the first two centuries AD. See Marcus Borg, *Meeting Jesus Again for the First Time: The Historical Jesus and the Heart of Contemporary Faith* (New York: HarperCollins, 2009).

14. Borg, *Reading the Bible Again*, 32.

approach, he notes, "Any document is sacred only because it is sacred *for a particular community*."[15] It is a mistake to substitute status for origin.

Both Gomes and Borg seem to want "thin places," "Pentecost experiences," and "sacramental space" without the life-altering, deconstructive otherness found in such spaces. Missing in both Gomes and Borg is the eclipse of the human subject. Both utilize the language of mystery, sacramental space, and Pentecost, but in the end, readers retain their role as final arbiters of truth. On the whole, however, they help move the conversation about the nature of the Bible into much-needed sacred space.

Hans Boersma

Hans Boersma offers an Evangelical vision of what he calls "the sacramental exegesis in the early church." His *ressourcement* project explores nine examples of patristic interpretation of Scripture. These examples illustrate "an ecclesial hermeneutic that treats Scripture as a sacrament containing a treasure of great value, Christ."[16]

Boersma is unabashedly a Christian Platonist: his worldview and theology sees everything as reflecting the glory and presence of God. Boersma distinguishes "between general sacramentality and the sacraments of the church." He writes, "The distinction between general and special revelation, between nature and grace, between world and church, is by no means theologically inconsequential."[17]

In keeping with Platonist thinking, Boersma understands that God's presence, specifically the presence of Christ, is non-direct and often hidden. He draws on patristic interpreters such as Origen to show how the ancient church understood the biblical text as a sacred depository for the *mysterium*—the mystery of Christ. Through the use of allegory, these writers helped uncover that sacred presence.

15. Borg, *Reading the Bible Again*, 29.

16. Hans Boersma, *Scripture as Real Presence: Sacramental Exegesis in the Early Church* (Grand Rapids: Baker Academic, 2017), 2.

17. Boersma, *Scripture as Real Presence*, 2.

Boersma's *ressourcement* project is a major step toward connecting the forgotten link between metaphysics and interpretation. Writes Boersma, "The way we think about the relationship between God and the world is immediately tied up with the way we read Scripture."[18] He, as well as the ancient writers, acknowledges a close connection between visible and invisible reality—the biblical text and the heavenly realms. This important move attempts to reconnect the natural and supernatural worlds that were torn apart during the rise of objective, natural science.

The key issues are how those worlds are connected and how the invisible world is to be known. The visible world, as seen in the Christian Platonist vision, contains "eternal patterns or 'forms' expressing themselves within the objects of the empirical world around us."[19] For Origen, the invisible spoken Word "becomes, as it were, flesh, when written in a book, clothed there by the letter's veil as it was by the veil of Jesus' flesh."[20]

For those of us who do not share Boersma's Neoplatonic worldview, some questions need to be answered. To what degree does the presence of the Holy Spirit unveil the mystery of Christ? How does one see the spiritual world in relation to the natural? What is the relationship between nature and sacrament? Is Scripture a bearer of a transcendent power or just an image of the "real world" of the transcendent? In the performance of the Scriptures—preaching and teaching—how directly is the presence of the triune life revealed? How does the Holy Spirit, through the reading of the Bible, bring us into the life of God?

Spiritual Reading

Richard Rohr

Roman Catholic mystic Richard Rohr is another example of someone seeking to reimage the Bible. For Rohr, "This marvelous anthology

18. Boersma, *Scripture as Real Presence*, 5.
19. Boersma, *Scripture as Real Presence*, 6.
20. Origen, *Homily on Leviticus* 1, as quoted in Telford Work, *Living and Active: Scripture in the Economy of Salvation* (Grand Rapids: Eerdmans, 2002), 27.

of books and letters called the Bible is all for the sake of astonishment! It's for divine transformation (*theōsis*), not intellectual or 'small-self' coziness."[21] He sees the problem with modern reading of the Bible as having made it into a "bunch of ideas." This Bible gives people answers but does not have the power to transform them.

Rohr seeks to place Scripture within a unified and mysterious cosmos, and much like Boersma, Rohr employs the concept of *mystērion* (1 Cor. 2:6–7:9) in imaging the Bible.[22] As mystery, the Bible is not something hidden, but it is "endlessly understandable. It is multilayered and pregnant with meaning and never totally admits to closure or resolution."[23] To read the Bible is, therefore, to enter the mysterious realm of Presence, wherein there is a sharing of the life and being of God.

Mystery is a key theme in Rohr's vision of the Bible. He declares that mystery is not something that is hidden as much as it is revealed. Respect for mystery allows the possibility of presence, "an encounter wherein the self-disclosure of one evokes a deeper life in the other."[24] Encountering the presence of God (God's gaze) creates a sense of being gathered into one place, where the fractured self is unified and made whole.

Eugene Peterson

Eugene Peterson's *Eat This Book: A Conversation in the Art of Spiritual Reading* is an example of an attempt to speak to the problem of the silence of the Bible in contemporary Christianity. "I want to pull the Christian Scriptures back from the margins of the contemporary imagination where they have been so rudely elbowed by their

21. Richard Rohr, *Things Hidden: Scripture as Spirituality* (Cincinnati: St. Anthony Messenger Press, 2007), 7.

22. The Greek word *mystērion* (secret rite, doctrine) was translated into two Latin words: *mysterium* and *sacramentum*. In the Roman Empire, *sacramentum* (sacred, holy) was a word used to signify a soldier's oath of allegiance. The ancient church adopted *sacramentum*, bringing together swearing allegiance to Christ as king as well as entry into the mysteries of Christ during the baptismal rite.

23. Rohr, *Things Hidden*, 62.

24. Rohr, *Things Hidden*, 64.

glamorous competitors and reestablish them at the center of the text for living the Christian life deeply and well."[25]

To do this, Peterson envisions reading the Bible as an "act of eating," meaning that reading is not an objective act but one of "taking it all in, assimilating it into the tissues of our lives."[26] For Peterson, revelation is deeply personal, revealing a God who is "relational to the core," so that "whatever is said, whatever is revealed, whatever is received is also personal and relational."[27] Peterson's statement resonates with the idea that enchantment is embedded in a relational cosmos. This personal nature of God defines the biblical text. It too is personal, and because it is personal it is also relational, requiring a personal, participatory reading.

Like Borg, Peterson advocates *lectio divina* as a "way of reading that guards against depersonalizing the text into an affair of questions and answers, definitions and dogmas." For him it is "a way of reading that intends the fusion of the entire biblical story and my story" and "a way that refuses to be reduced to *just* reading but intends the living of the text, listening and responding to the voices of that 'so great a cloud of witnesses.'"[28]

Peterson's insistence on the need for "fusion of the entire biblical story and my story" relates to Rohr's idea of the Cosmic Egg. The Cosmic Egg is an analogy for "three domes of meaning. The smallest dome of meaning is my private story. . . . The second and larger dome of meaning that encloses the first is 'This is us,' 'Our story.' . . . The third dome of meaning that encloses and regulates the two smaller ones is called 'The Story.'"[29] Two significant differences between Peterson and Rohr are that Rohr inserts group identity as a second hermeneutical layer and expands the Story to include Scripture as well as truths beyond Scripture.

25. Eugene Peterson, *Eat This Book: A Conversation in the Art of Spiritual Reading* (Grand Rapids: Eerdmans, 2006), 17.
26. Peterson, *Eat This Book*, 17.
27. Peterson, *Eat This Book*, 20.
28. Peterson, *Eat This Book*, 90.
29. Rohr, *Things Hidden*, 21–23.

The Bible in the Economy of Salvation

John Webster

Perhaps one of the most promising attempts to re-enchant the text is represented in John Webster's *Holy Scripture*. Writing from the context of British Anglicanism, Webster attempts to place the biblical text within the economy of God's communicative grace. As such, he seeks to return the Bible to its rightful place in the context of revelation, taking it from the sterile discussions on the inspiration of Scripture. For Webster, "The inspiration of Scripture needs to be strictly subordinate to and dependent upon the broader concept of revelation."[30] Revelation as the self-presentation of the triune God is indeed the divine presence of God. In this context, Scripture has an ontological status of "sanctified creature." As such, Scripture serves the purposes of God's divine self-disclosure. It is set aside in the divine service of bringing about "the communicative economy of God's merciful friendship with his lost creatures."[31]

For Webster, the sanctification of Scripture "is not to be restricted to the text as a finished product; it may legitimately be extended to the larger field of agents and actions of which the text is a part, . . . the complex histories of pre-literary and literary tradition, redaction and compilation. It will, likewise, be extended to the post-history of the text, most particularly to canonization . . . and interpretation (understood as Spirit-illumined repentant and faithful attention to the presence of God)."[32]

Webster removes Scripture from the modernist context of "first principle," from which other doctrines (e.g., the doctrine of God) are derived, and returns it to its rightful place within discussions of the economy of God. By doing so, he makes it possible to reintroduce pneumatological language and to go beyond the Spirit's role in inspiration. The biblical text, as sanctified vessel, becomes a vehicle

30. John Webster, *Holy Scripture: A Dogmatic Sketch* (Cambridge: Cambridge University Press, 2003), 72.

31. Webster, *Holy Scripture*, 29.

32. Webster, *Holy Scripture*, 29–30.

for the *actual presence* of the triune God. Sanctification includes readers who, by the Spirit, are taken into the economy of God's grace.

Of all the writers I have mentioned, Webster has the most robust pneumatology. He sees the Holy Spirit as offering a "divine moving" of God into the realm of the text. This moving does not mean that the text in its static form is something that was "moved upon" by God but means that, in actuality, it is "a text that has within it a very present divine mark."[33] Furthermore, the work of the Spirit in the text is tied to God's economy of saving grace. Thus to read the Bible is "to be slain and made alive," and it "can only occur as a kind of brokenness, a relinquishment of willed mastery of the text."[34]

Telford Work

Telford Work seeks to develop an "economic Trinitarian theology of Scripture" that "continually revisits bibliology in light of every other locus of theology. A systematic, trinitarian doctrine of Scripture is necessarily circular: all the categories that describe it also emerge from it. This circularity liberates the doctrine of Scripture from its prolegomenal ghetto and appreciates the Bible as reaching into the very plan of God and the very heart of the Christian life."[35] Noting the relationship between God's character and God's Word, Work writes, "If Scripture is God's Word, then in some sense it reflects God's character, and if God's character is Triune, then the Bible reflects the triunity of God in some significant way."[36]

Like Webster, Work sees Scripture playing a role in the divine economy of salvation. In addition, he sees Scripture as conferring and reflecting the character of the church. Work believes the Bible as Word of God suggests a trinitarian ontology of Scripture, the Bible's role in salvation history suggests a soteriology of Scripture, and the Bible's

33. Webster, *Holy Scripture*, 36.
34. Webster, *Holy Scripture*, 88.
35. Telford Work, *Living and Active: Scripture in the Economy of Salvation* (Grand Rapids: Eerdmans, 2002), 9.
36. Work, *Living and Active*, 10.

relationship with the church suggests an ecclesiology of Scripture. Overall, the Bible offers a "bibliology from above" as well as a "bibliology from below," a "synthetic divine-human perspective of *koinōnia* between God and humanity in an eternal 'descent' and 'ascent.'"[37]

Both Webster and Work seek to remove the Bible as first principle and bring it back into its rightful place as a vessel in the life of God's economy. In doing so, they offer a way beyond seemingly endless hermeneutical and epistemological discussions about biblical interpretation.

The Otherness of Holy Scripture

In the hands of modernity, the Bible lost a large degree of its subjecthood; it became real estate, an object to be bought, sold, analyzed, and, unfortunately, sometimes used as a weapon. One of our tasks today is to recover a vision of the Bible with the centrifugal power of otherness, as Scripture.

Karl Barth

In the twentieth century Karl Barth strove to wrestle the Bible out of its entrapment as an object under the control of human interpreters and to place it back into the realm of God. For Barth, the Bible represented otherness, a "strange, new world, the world of God."[38] He developed a triadic framework: Jesus Christ as Word of God in first form, Scripture as Word of God in second form, and the church's proclamation of the Word as the third form.[39]

For Barth, these three forms exist as a *vestigium trinitatis*, the only true vestige of the Trinity available to humankind.[40] Writes Work, "For

37. Work, *Living and Active*, 10.

38. Karl Barth, "The Strange New World within the Bible," in *The Word of God and the Word of Man*, trans. Douglas Horton (Gloucester, MA: Peter Smith, 1978), 33.

39. Karl Barth, *Church Dogmatics*, vol. I/2, *The Doctrine of the Word of God*, trans. G. W. Bromiley, ed. G. W. Bromiley and T. G. Torrance (New York: T&T Clark, 2004), 111–21. For an insightful discussion of Barth's threefold treatment of the Word of God, see Work, *Living and Active*, 67–100.

40. Barth, *Church Dogmatics* I/1, 121.

Barth, the writtenness of Holy Writ corresponds to its humanity, its holiness to its divinity. Barth clearly understand this as a Christological analogy for Scripture. Thus, the Bible is not half-human and half-divine; it is fully both."[41]

While Barth's formulation of the Bible as second form of Word may be helpful in moving toward trinitarian dimensions, it is not helpful in developing a full trinitarian ontology of Scripture. In the end, Barth reflects a christological focus at the expense of pneumatology. As Work notes, "In the Bible's own witness Jesus Christ is not *one form of the logos*, but the Logos himself." Furthermore, Work notes, "The Bible usually discusses Scripture not in terms of the Son, but in terms of the Holy Spirit. The most direct texts on the nature of Scripture, 2 Timothy 3:16 and 2 Peter 1:20–21, treat Scripture not as *logikos* [speech/reasoning] but as *theopneustos* [God-breathed]."[42]

Joel Green

To read the Bible as Scripture is to testify to its otherness. It is also to testify to its power. Joel Green points out the astonishing irony of how references to Barth's understanding of the Bible as a "strange, new world, the world of God," have morphed into a "*historical* definition of the Bible's strangeness." In doing so, interpreters have equated otherness with distance, thereby missing the point altogether. While otherness does exist in the distance of time, customs, and culture, the Bible's primary otherness lies in its capacity as Subject: it has a "performative capacity to act."[43]

For Green, "Reading the Bible as Scripture accords privilege to the role of this text in divine self-disclosure."[44] He laments that far too often the Bible is approached as merely a compilation of texts and not as Christian Scripture. "The Bible as Scripture" is first and

41. Work, *Living and Active*, 73.

42. Work, *Living and Active*, 78–79.

43. Joel Green, *Seized by Truth: Reading the Bible as Scripture* (Nashville: Abingdon, 2007), 156.

44. Green, *Seized by Truth*, 11.

foremost a theological statement that points to these writings' origin in God's revelation.

Green's concern is how scientific methods objectify the biblical texts to the degree that their otherness is co-opted into human capacity to interpret them. The Bible, if condemned to history, lacks the power to transform readers. The way out of this dilemma is to locate Scripture within the framework of Pentecost.

According to Green, the Pentecost Spirit generates the church's interpreting of Scripture and forms a community shaped by the proclaimed Word. He envisions a "reading of Scripture that is ecclesially located, theologically fashioned, critically engaged, and Spirit imbued."[45]

Green's vision of a Pentecost reading of the text is grounded in a foundational view of Scripture that Peter Gomes's vision of Pentecost lacks. In addition, Green's reading is more ecclesially grounded. However, like Gomes, Green fails to discuss the unique ontology of the Bible within the frame of Pentecost, especially the Bible's status as pneumatologically formed and sustained such that it reveals the life of God.

Green writes, "If we give ourselves to the life of the Spirit and engagement with Scripture, God so works in our lives and imaginations that we are led further into the biblical narrative, so that we find the Bible more and more to be true." The way to get to this place is to be "deeply embedded in faithful communities of discipleship, people in whom the Spirit is actualizing the Word of God, and thus, for whom the Word of God is authenticated."[46]

In the end, Green sees the Spirit at work in communities of faith and in individuals by actualizing the Word of God. He fails to delve into the metaphysical and ontological nature of the biblical text. Just how does the Spirit work uniquely in and through the Bible?

Wesley Kort

Wesley Kort points out that the postliberal approach to reading the Bible grants "a new confidence to religious communities and

45. Green, *Seized by Truth*, 101.
46. Green, *Seized by Truth*, 164.

confirms the force and significance of their languages and practices."[47] However, Kort says, "These positions subject reading the Bible to perspectives and practices that arise from and are characteristic of the institution or occasion that forms reading's context. They are positions that subsume reading the Bible under a set of interests that determine how the Bible will be read, what it means to read the Bible 'as . . .'"[48] In other words, reading of the Bible is primarily centripetal.

For Kort, deconstruction reasserts the Bible *as Scripture*. It frames the text, as John Calvin did, in a centrifugal manner, recognizing "the distance and the uncertainty that always exist between the reader and the saving knowledge that may be received in and by reading scripture." Kort continues: "Where there is no question that reading can always be dominated by already formulated cognitive and institutional conclusions, it is precisely the possibility of delivery from such domination that reading the Bible as scripture holds out."[49]

Kort points out that while a centripetal reading of the Bible was "absolutely crucial for Calvin, he does not end here. Calvin's theory of reading Scripture also contains a centrifugal moment, one that moves from saving knowledge outward not only to the whole of Scripture but to the relation of Scripture to the whole of life."[50] In this sense, for Calvin, the otherness of Scripture did not merely mean a vertical relationship. Rather, it was decentering while at the same time serving the purpose of orienting and grounding a community.

Kort also draws from postmodern theorists Maurice Blanchot and Julia Kristeva, both of whom oppose modern ways of reading and, in Kort's view, offer possibilities of a centrifugal reading of the Bible. Blanchot points out how modern reading mirrors our culture's addiction to answers: "Answers dominate and set the conditions of

47. Wesley Kort, *"Take, Read": Scripture, Textuality, and Cultural Practice* (University Park: Pennsylvania State University Press, 1996), 121.
48. Kort, *"Take, Read,"* 122.
49. Kort, *"Take, Read,"* 122–23.
50. Kort, *"Take, Read,"* 30.

the culture because answers resemble commodities and appeal to the cultural desire to possess. . . . Answers and commodities become possessions and are stored."[51] Even more dangerous, Kort says, is the fact that, "since our culture is one of accumulation and possession, the culturally prestigious act of learning, rather than stand[ing] apart, is subsumed by the ethos of grasping and hoarding and grants that ethos legitimacy."[52] Translating this ethos into Christian circles, study of the Bible becomes one more means of accumulation, a way of preserving the self rather than divesting of the self.

Kort does not intend to offer an ontology of the Bible; his interest is in the act of reading. However, in his insistence on the deconstructing, centrifugal power of the biblical text, Kort points in the direction of naming the nature of this strange otherness and how this otherness is our hope for re-enchantment.

Recent discussions on the nature of Scripture contain a common thread of seeing the Bible as more than a flat text or a historical artifact. These scholars, each in their own way, are seeking to define the meaning of *more*. The Bible is *more* because it offers a thin place, a threshold where two worlds meet. The Bible is *more* because it offers the sacramental power to mediate divine presence. The Bible is *more* because it provides a means toward sharing in the life of God. The Bible is *more* because it is a sanctified vessel of God's economy of salvation. The Bible is *more* because it offers a radical otherness, one of divine self-disclosure and centrifugal power.

I see all the above coming together within the framework of Pentecost. Like Green, I understand Pentecost as the hermeneutical key for a reading of Scripture, one that offers the possibility of radical transformation. But, going beyond Green, I wish to explore Pentecost as the key to defining the ontological nature of Scripture. It is my understanding that the Feast of Pentecost offered the fulfillment

51. Maurice Blanchot, *The Infinite Conversation* (L'entretien infini), trans. Susan Hanson (Minneapolis: University of Minnesota Press, 1993), 13, as quoted in Kort, "*Take, Read,*" 98.

52. Kort, "*Take, Read,*" 96.

of Jesus's reconciling mission. Pentecost is the enchanting feast that brings it all together: heaven and earth, God and humanity, flesh and spirit, Jews and gentiles, sons and daughters, young and old. The question that begs to be answered is this: What role does the Bible play in this grand reunion?

6

The Enchanting Festival of Pentecost

Enchantment involves a unified cosmology wherein harmony and deep relationships flourish. An enchanted world creates space for the flourishing of the imagination and provides a space to play. Enchantment offers the radical pull of otherness, granting wonder as well as the possibility of deconstruction. All these aspects come together in the great Feast of Pentecost.

Pentecost is symbolically and historically related to the Jewish harvest Festival of Shavuot (Feast of Weeks), which commemorates the giving of the law at Sinai; this feast also celebrates the wheat harvest. Pentecost thus uniquely ties together creation and history: the harvest and the giving of the law at Horeb. The grain harvest lasted seven weeks and was a season of gladness (Deut. 16:9–11; Isa. 9:2; Jer. 5:24). This season began with the harvesting of barley during Passover and ended with the wheat harvest at Shavuot. This day was a time when people could bring the firstfruits to the temple in Jerusalem. They would load baskets of the harvest on oxen, whose horns were gilded and laced with garlands of flowers. These oxen would lead the procession to Jerusalem, accompanied by music and festive parade. In contemporary Jewish celebration, synagogues are decorated with greenery and beautiful flowers. Some place a canopy of greenery over the place where the scrolls are read.[1]

For Christians, Pentecost is observed fifty days after Easter, and it celebrates the descent of the Holy Spirit upon the 120 disciples as recorded in Acts 2. It is appropriate that both green and red are the liturgical colors of Pentecost: green in the Eastern churches and red in the Western churches. In the tradition of the midrash, Horeb bloomed with flowers in anticipation of the giving of the Torah.[2] Here we can see the red (fire) and the green (blooming plants) coming together.

In Christianity, the Orthodox tradition continues to tie Pentecost to Shavuot. Because they regard the church as having existed before the creation of the world, Orthodox believers do not see Pentecost as the birthday of the church.[3] Rather, it signifies the fulfillment of the mission of Christ and the beginning of the messianic age of the kingdom of God. In Eastern Europe, Pentecost is a holiday during which houses and churches are decorated with greenery. In some places, processions are made to the fields, where the crops are blessed.

Eastern churches celebrate with an all-night vigil, known as the Service of Kneeling Prayer, on the eve of Pentecost. The Orthodox tradition of Pentecost contains a remarkable gestalt of nature and grace, history and creation. It unifies the fires of Horeb—and the tongues of fire in the upper room—with the bounty of harvest. In the rituals surrounding the feast, the full meaning of the book of Joel is enacted: calls for lament and repentance, followed by God's promises of restoring creation and pouring out the Spirit upon

1. This summary is taken from Tamar Yeomans, "Shavu'ot—Feast of Weeks," Beit Gan-Eden, https://www.bgemc.org/shavursquoot-pentecost.html.

2. See "Shavuot: What Is Shavuot, When Is Shavuot, Shavuot Meaning and Importance," AlephBeta, https://www.alephbeta.org/shavuot/what-is-shavuot.

3. See, e.g, Shepherd of Hermas, Vision 2.4 [8].1.

all flesh. What many Christians overlook is how the promises of Joel reveal that in the coming of the Spirit, all life is vivified and renewed.

The Icon of Pentecost

The Icon of Pentecost depicts the outpouring of the Holy Spirit upon the apostles, who were present with others in the upper room. Paul is included in the image because he too was filled with the Spirit and became an apostle. The apostles are seated in a circle. Paul holds a book. The other apostles each hold a scroll. The book and the scrolls convey that the writings of the apostles, including Paul, are to be seen as rooted in the coming of the Holy Spirit, fulfilling Jesus's promise that even though he would be leaving them, he was sending the Paraclete, the Spirit of Truth.

The mythic figure of Cosmos stands in the bottom center of the icon. He is emerging from darkness, and his hands carry a white cloth upon which sit twelve scrolls, representing the teaching of the apostles. Cosmos is wearing a crown, but he is not crowned with the glory that surrounds the heads of the apostles. Rather, his crown is

Figure 6.1 An icon of the Christian Pentecost in the Russian Orthodox tradition.

a worldly one worn by the kings of the earth. Cosmos represents the fallen order, all nations and all people who are bound under the curse of sin. In the icon's depiction of Cosmos, there is a sense that it is both tarnished and beautiful, portraying a worn dignity. Cosmos is aging, yet he is emerging into a newly born era in which light overcomes darkness, and order overcomes chaos.

Unified Cosmology

The Icon of Pentecost reveals metaphysics in which, on the ascension of Christ and the pouring out of the Spirit, heaven and earth are once again united. It portends a flourishing ecology in which the cosmos, having been held captive in darkness, is released from its prison and able to come forth into the light.

The icon depicts a pneumatic cosmology, one in which there is a unified ethos of the spiritual and material worlds. In this image, heaven meets earth and the whole of the cosmos receives the light of the new creation.[4] A pneumatic cosmology is filled with mystery. The Icon of Pentecost indicates the invitation surrounding the mystery of the incarnation. Writes Diogenes Allen, "Mysteries to be known must be entered into." He goes on to note, "For we do not solve mysteries, we enter into them. The deeper we enter into them, the more illumination we get. Still greater depths are revealed to us the further we go."[5] As the apostle Paul writes, "With all wisdom and insight, he has made known to us the mystery of his will, according to his good pleasure that he set forth in Christ, as a plan for the fullness of time, to gather up all things in him, things in heaven and things on earth" (Eph. 1:8–10).

Pentecost did not solve the mystery of Christ, in the sense of one solving a hidden problem. Rather, this festival opened the way for us to *enter into* the mystery once hidden from us. Furthermore, the whole

4. In the recent *First Nations Version: An Indigenous Translation of the New Testament* (Downers Grove, IL: IVP Books, 2021), "Creator Sets Free" is the name given to Jesus. This name beautifully depicts the cosmic mission of Christ.

5. Diogenes Allen, *Temptation* (New York: Seabury Classics, 2004), 6–7.

cosmos is freed from its dark prison and is now able to move into the light of the glorious mystery. Paul's Epistle to the Colossians beautifully portrays this scene: "I became its servant according to God's commission that was given to me for you, to make the word of God fully known, the mystery that has been hidden throughout the ages and generations but has now been revealed to his saints. To them God chose to make known how great among the Gentiles are the riches of glory of this mystery, which is Christ in you, the hope of glory" (1:25–27).

Notice that in this text the "word of God" is closely tied to "the mystery that has been hidden throughout the ages." It is the word of God that serves as the means of revealing the mystery of Christ. King Cosmos holds in his hands the scrolls containing the "word of God," and it is this word that is liberating him from darkness.

Paul reminds the Colossians that he is not the only steward of this great mystery. It is now being revealed to the saints, including the gentiles. The saints receive within themselves Christ, the great mystery and the hope of glory. Just as the icon depicts Cosmos being delivered from the darkness, Paul reminds his readers that we have been rescued from "the power of darkness and transferred . . . into the kingdom of his beloved son, in whom we have redemption, the forgiveness of sin" (1:12–13).

Paul paints a beautiful image of the cosmic Christ, the one in whom "all things in heaven and on earth were created, things visible and invisible; . . . all things have been created through him and for him" (Col. 1:16). The coming of the Spirit at Pentecost is the reconciling of *all things* because Christ's death made "peace through the blood of his cross" (v. 20).

Cosmic Harmony

Pentecost is a festival celebrating creation being set free and things long separated being reunited: heaven and earth, God and humanity, Jews and gentiles, male and female, slave and free. It's a grand party where everything and everyone sings in harmony. Eugene Peterson captures this imagery well in his translation of Colossians 1:20: "But all the broken and dislocated pieces of the universe—people and things, animals and atoms—get properly fixed and fit together in vibrant harmonies" (The Message).

Acts 2 gives a vivid description of things getting properly fixed and fit together: "When the day of Pentecost had come, they were all together in one place. And suddenly from heaven there came a sound like the rush of a violent wind, and it filled the entire house where they were sitting. Divided tongues, as of fire, appeared among them, and a tongue rested on each of them. All of them were filled with the Holy Spirit and began to speak in other languages, as the Spirit gave them ability" (vv. 1–4). Those present in Jerusalem, "devout Jews from every nation under heaven" (Acts 2:5), were drawn to the spectacle. They were amazed and astonished because they heard common people speaking in the languages of all these different nations. Peter, taking advantage of the crowd's astonishment, began to preach. In his sermon, he tied this spectacle to the prophecy of Joel—namely, the pouring out of the Spirit upon all flesh as well as cosmic signs in the heavens (Joel 2:28–32).

Within the framework of Pentecost, therefore, Word, Spirit, and flesh unite to proclaim the good news of God's grand cosmic ingathering. Human tongues speak in many languages, "as the Spirit gave them ability" (Acts 2:4). What appears to be babble, a cacophony of voices, is a sign of humanity in harmonious worship.

This scene is also one of natural elements—wind and fire—uniting with humanity in enchanting harmony. Recall Hildegard of Bingen's understanding of cosmic harmony. Her theology of the cosmos included a description of how each of the elements possessed the "pristine sound that it had at the time of creation." She wrote, "Fire has flames and sings in praise of God. Wind whistles a hymn to God as it fans the flames. And the human voice consists of words to sing paeans of praise. All creation is a single hymn in praise to God."[6] At

6. Hildegard of Bingen, *Analecta Sacra*, vol. 8, ed. J. B. Pitra (Monte Cassino, 1882), 352, as quoted in Heinrich Schipperges, *Hildegard of Bingen: Healing and the Nature of the Cosmos*, trans. John A. Broadwin (Princeton: Markus Wiener, 1998), 27.

Pentecost, flames of fire joined with wind; these elements united with human voices in a single hymn of praise to God. Such a wonder had not occurred since the fall. In my Pentecostal imaginary, I see angels and heavenly beings joining themselves to this enchanted wonder.

The cosmic harmony of Pentecost serves as an eschatological sign of the end, a time beautifully described in John's Apocalypse:

> After this I looked, and there was a great multitude that no one could count, from every nation, from all tribes and peoples and languages, standing before the throne and before the Lamb, robed in white, with palm branches in their hands. They cried out in a loud voice, saying,
>
> "Salvation belongs to our God who is seated on the throne,
> and to the Lamb!"
>
> And all the angels stood around the throne and around the elders and the four living creatures, and they fell on their faces before the throne and worshiped God, singing,
>
> "Amen! Blessing and glory and wisdom
> and thanksgiving and honor
> and power and might
> be to our God forever and ever! Amen."
>
> (Rev. 7:9–12)

Pentecost as Outpouring of Divine Love

Pentecost signifies the giving of the law at Horeb. It also signifies the joys of the restored embrace between God and his people, an embrace made possible by the cross. Pentecost brings together things that were long disjointed, creating a beautiful harmony. This harmony reflects a stream of deep relationality, one fueled by the flames of divine love. The baptism of the Holy Spirit on the day of Pentecost was a baptism of love. The fire at Pentecost contained flames of love, burning away the distancing shame present since the fall.

The Holy Spirit came upon the flesh of Mary, giving birth to the incarnation of God's love. At Pentecost, the Spirit came upon flesh, granting those gathered the gift of embodied agape (Greek: *agapē*). Caroline Redick dialogues with Charles Taylor's understanding of agape to develop her argument that agape serves as a strong moral source.[7] By participating in agape love, persons are "fitted together in a dissymmetric proportionality, . . . which comes from God . . . and which became possible because God became flesh."[8]

Building upon Taylor, Redick examines the third article of the Trinity as a way of investigating the meaning of participating in agape. She describes the relationality of Pentecost as "*agapic* participation." Writes Redick, "Through the Spirit of love, human persons take part in divine love, sharing in what properly belongs to the Godhead without exhausting it."[9] For Redick, the outpouring of love at Pentecost created and continues to create a deeply participatory ontology, a way of being in the world that has the power to cross boundaries of kinship, gender, ethnicity, and social hierarchy.[10]

A tenth-century midrash quotes Rabbi Akiva as saying, "Had Torah not been given, it would have been possible to conduct the world on the basis of the Song of Songs alone." Rabbi Akiva also states, "All of Scripture is holy, but the Song of Songs is the Holy of Holies."[11] In light of this rabbinic saying, we might envision Pentecost as the marriage of the Torah and the Song of Songs. It is the celebration of the law being written on human hearts as well as a time of God's lavishing his love on humanity. Throughout history, mystics have picked up the imagery of the Song of Songs as a way of articu-

7. Caroline Redick, "Spirit Baptism as a Moral Source in a Secular Age," *Pneuma* 40 (2018): 35–57.

8. Charles Taylor, *A Secular Age* (Cambridge, MA: Harvard University Press, 2007), 739, as quoted in Redick, "Spirit Baptism," 49. See also Taylor, *Sources of the Self: The Making of the Modern Identity* (Cambridge, MA: Harvard University Press, 1989).

9. Redick, "Spirit Baptism," 51.

10. Redick, "Spirit Baptism," 56.

11. Quoted in Arthur Green, "I Have Come to My Garden," *Jewish Review of Books*, Fall 2015, https://jewishreviewofbooks.com/articles/1874/i-have-come-to-my-garden/.

lating intimacy of life in Christ. Dale Coulter writes that Richard of St. Victor, in his short work *On the Four Degrees of Violent Charity*, described the "ecstatic embrace" of Christ's love as "a ravishing of the soul by Christ."[12]

The love poured out at Pentecost is an act of grace. John Wesley understood grace, says Coulter, "in trinitarian terms as the favor of the Father expressed in the Son and the power of the Spirit given through the Son. The former represents the love of God for us while the latter is the love of God in us."[13]

Pneumatic Imagination

The descent of the Holy Spirit at Pentecost not only brings about the gift of divine love, it also facilitates and transforms the human imagination. "The Holy Spirit is God's imagination let loose and working with all the freedom of God in the world, and in the lives, the words and actions, of the men and women of our time," writes John McIntyre.[14] Pentecost provided a baptism of God's imaginative Spirit, enabling humanity to envision a new world. Peter's sermon on the day of Pentecost was an imaginative leap, one that tied together Joel's prophecies with what was taking place in Jerusalem many years later. By the Spirit, Peter was able to see a new creation, one that was ordered in a radically different way than the one in which he lived. Peter's vision was of a world being reclaimed by the cosmic Christ. A new era was unfolding, one in which the Holy Spirit is poured into *all flesh*—women and men, slave and free. Fragile clay vessels are now able to house heaven's treasures.

The pneumatic imaginary of Pentecost is open. King Cosmos emerges from the darkness because the "entire cosmos . . . is porous

12. Dale M. Coulter, "The Unfolding Love of Spirit Baptism," *Firebrand*, June 15, 2021, https://firebrandmag.com/articles/the-unfolding-love-of-spirit-baptism.

13. Coulter, "Unfolding Love."

14. John McIntyre, "New Help from Kant: Theology and Human Imagination," in *Religious Imagination*, ed. James P. Mackey (Edinburgh: Edinburgh University Press, 1987), 64.

and healable."[15] Daniela Augustine describes the Orthodox imaginary of Pentecost as the "assertion of Pentecost as the very goal/purpose of the Incarnation (and the anticipated theotic pneumatization of both humanity and the rest of the cosmos)—grasping that all of creation in its materiality (including the human body) is made in, by and for the Spirit, and the Church as 'communion of the Holy Spirit' is the visible expression of creation's pneumatic *telos*."[16]

In anticipation of the fulfillment of Jesus's promise to send the Holy Spirit, those gathered on that day tarried together, making themselves open and available for this gift. Their openness was anticipatory and hopeful. It involved waiting and longing. They knew that the room in which they were gathered was porous space. They had seen the risen Jesus walk though closed doors. His Spirit could do the same. An ordinary room was soon to become the center of cosmic space.

"The Holy Spirit is God's imagination let loose and working with all the freedom of God in the world," writes Amos Yong.[17] Building upon his definition of the imagination as worldmaking, Yong envisions the Spirit's role in worldmaking as the "pneumatological imagination." He understands the pneumatological imagination going about the task of worldmaking at three levels. First, "it recognizes that whatever there is to be encountered is multi-dimensional at least insofar as it is a result of being acted upon as well as being a creative and more-or-less powerful actor in its own right." Within the world are "various powers acting and being acted upon." Second, the "pneumatological imagination engages the worldmaking process holistically, combining valuational, affective, and spiritual sensitivities to the task." In this task, the Spirit is at work with people and

15. Wolfgang Vondey, "Religion at Play: Pentecostalism and the Transformation of the Secular Age," *Pneuma* 40 (2019): 28.

16. Daniela Christova Augustine, "Where the Spirit Dwells: Reflections on 'The Encyclical of the Recent Holy and Great Council of the Orthodox Church' through an Eastern-European Pentecostal Lens," *Journal of World Christianity* 11, no. 1 (2021): 7.

17. Amos Yong, *Spirit-Word-Community: Theological Hermeneutics in Trinitarian Perspective* (Eugene, OR: Wipf & Stock, 2002), 18.

"alert to the paradoxical interconnectedness of the knowing self with the objects to be known." Third, the pneumatological imagination engages in the task of worldmaking at two levels: discernment and engagement. The "pneumatological imagination enables the kind of honesty which identifies, names, and resists all that the scriptures declare to be 'of the flesh,' of the 'form of the world,' and the demonic."[18]

The imaginative Spirit of Pentecost makes a world in which the ethos of the kingdom of God flourishes. In this world, the last are first, and the first are last. The spectacle of the upper room drew a crowd. All were amazed that common Galileans were speaking in the languages of the ancient world (Acts 2:7). Some sneered at the spectacle, saying, "They are filled with new wine" (v. 13). Since its inception, the "all-flesh" social imaginary of Pentecost has mocked the order of empires.

In the early part of the twentieth century, the Azusa Street revival, led by William Seymour, the son of formerly enslaved people, became the object of intense criticism. In the era of Jim Crow, the sight of Black, White, Hispanic, and Asian people all worshiping together was scandalous. Reporters from the *Los Angeles Times* enjoyed writing scathing criticisms and drawing outlandish cartoons of those gathered at the Azusa Mission. As with the events in Jerusalem, others were drawn to the power of the new community. Well-dressed White businessmen were drawn into the embrace of Black women domestic workers. They danced together in the Spirit. Seymour hoped that Azusa would be the beginning of America's color line being erased. For a while, this seemed possible; but over the course of time, Azusa's sheer excess of gift and its imagination of radical inclusion became too much for many to hold.

The world created at Pentecost was not only one of inverted social order but also one that reversed the fund of knowledge. No longer was knowledge to be the exclusive real estate of the educated and the elite. Pentecost epistemology offers knowledge of God, the writing of God's law on human hearts. Along with knowledge, it bestows the

18. Yong, *Spirit-Word-Community*, 146–49.

gifts of wisdom and discernment. This fund of knowledge was so powerful that it later caused Tertullian to ask the rhetorical question, What does Jerusalem have to do with Athens?[19]

A Pentecost imaginary does not suspend reason; rather, it offers the possibility for the transrational. The gift of Pentecost opens space for the depths of the human mind to be set free from the constraints of a fallen world, for us to be able to know as we are known. In the words of Nimi Wariboko, "Knowledge is a metaphysics of the presence of God; the supreme being is present without mediation, a secure ground of thought that is proper to knowledge and meaning, is good and self-identical, correct and pure, and not secondary, derivative, or complicated."[20] This is the type of epistemology in which someone might say "to make spirit" over against "to make sense."

Wariboko sees this form of Pentecost knowledge circumventing the logic of Babel, the preeminent display of human sense lifting itself to reach God. In Pentecost, God is reaching out to lift humanity; in this space, knowledge is gift. As in the story of Babel, human reason alone has led to some tragic choices. The phrase "it makes sense" has been applied to all sorts of human atrocities. Writes Wariboko, "The power of spirit is neither pure reason nor pure irrationality. It is to hold the constructedness of reason or sense to the demands of the event of human flourishing. It is to sense the gap between what reason offers on the basis of the present order or being and what is to come, the order of the to-come (Rev. 1:8)."[21] The reasoning of Pentecost has an eschatological flavor that brings the future to bear on the present.

It is important to note that Pentecost is an event of embodiment, one in which the divine and the natural coinhere. It offers an embodied way of knowing as well as an embodied ontology. This festival skillfully weaves together Spirit, the natural elements of fire and wind, and human bodies. The Spirit filled people, loosing their tongues and granting them languages beyond their capabilities.

19. Tertullian, *Prescription against Heretics* 7.

20. Nimi Wariboko, *The Pentecostal Hypothesis: Christ Talks, They Decide* (Eugene, OR: Cascade Books, 2020), xiv.

21. Wariboko, *Pentecostal Hypothesis*, 140.

Pentecost is not a festival of escapism. Neither is it a festival of extreme intervention, one in which the supernatural world temporarily overwhelms the natural world and then departs back into the "other realm." The natural world, in the words of James K. A. Smith, is "already *primed* for the Spirit's manifestations." Smith's "participatory ontology," in dialogue with Radical Orthodoxy, sees the natural world as created and suspended from the transcendent Creator. The transcendent inheres in immanence.[22] Amos Yong adds a "pneumatological assist" to this participatory ontology. The Holy Spirit is the agent of this suspension, "the triune person in whom the material world is suspended."[23]

While the natural world, including human beings, is already primed for the Spirit's manifestation, it has been marred and disenchanted to the degree that it required the coming of Christ and the pouring out of the Spirit to break the spell of disenchantment. To this day we sometimes require intense interventions of the Spirit to remind us of our enchanted status as beings held and suspended from the transcendent-immanent Creator.

Pentecost as Imaginative Play

The contemporary haunting and longing for enchantment includes a deep desire for free, imaginative space. Both Burning Man and *Sleep No More* (see chap. 3) regularly draw thousands of people, especially young adults, into a space where they can, for a time, suspend the rules of ordinary life and imaginatively play.[24]

The space created by Pentecost facilitates freedom of play. As Amy Spittler Shaffer writes, "Kids dance on the quantum froth, and we call it 'play' because we don't have a good word for it, or an understanding

22. James K. A. Smith, *Thinking in Tongues: Pentecostal Contributions to Christian Philosophy* (Grand Rapids: Eerdmans, 2010), 100.

23. Amos Yong, "Radically Orthodox, Reformed, and Pentecostal: Rethinking the Intersection of Post/Modernity and the Religions in Conversation with James K. A. Smith," *Journal of Pentecostal Theology* 15 (2007): 246.

24. I have referenced Pentecost as the festival that evangelizes the Nones. See Cheryl Bridges Johns, "Preaching Pentecost to the Nones," *Journal for Preachers* 36, no. 4 (2013): 3–10.

infinite enough to reflect what is really occurring."[25] Pentecost reflects imaginative free space wherein the divine is at play *with* the natural world in a manner that resolves the tension between the two. Pentecost is "the playful, irrational, unexpected, and foolish markers of the kingdom of God breaking into the secular." Vondey describes this experience as a time when the "realm of the 'charismatic' cuts through the 'secular' and muddles the distinction between transcendence and immanence and what belongs to each realm." It is when "charismatic time ticks within a 'perichoretic' cosmos."[26]

It's an irony that among the world's poor is where the most exuberant free-play expressions of Pentecost can be found. People living in places characterized by poverty and violence, whose lives by external appearances have little to celebrate, are often the most celebratory and free. During most of the twentieth century it was common to dismiss ecstatic worship among the poor as an opiate or a form of escapism. These interpretive grids missed the internal dynamics of such communities. Rather than escaping from the world, people invite the chaos and pain of daily life into the sacred circle where, in the light of the Presence, such things lose their power.

The metaphor of jazz, which invites human participation and innovation, can be used to interpret the aesthetics of Pentecost. Jennifer Gosetti-Ferencei describes jazz as having "spontaneous improvisation, and its further promotion of creativity." Jazz creates a space for free play, for creative consciousness that by its nature is "both situated and transcending."[27] These two blend together through improvisation. Improvisation involves "reworking pre-composed materials and design in relation to unanticipated ideas conceived, shaped, and performed under the special conditions of performance, thereby adding unique features to every creation."[28]

25. Amy Spittler Shaffer, "The Wonderment: How It Works," *The Wonderment*, 2017, https://thewonderment.com/how-it-works.

26. Vondey, "Religion at Play," 26.

27. Jennifer Anna Gosetti-Ferencei, *The Life of Imagination* (New York: Columbia University Press, 2018), 238.

28. Paul F. Berliner, *Thinking in Jazz: The Infinite Art of Improvisation* (Chicago: University of Chicago Press, 1994), 241.

In Pentecost, people are not seized by a transcendent realm and forced into a way of being in which they have lost control. Neither is Pentecost a space of tight ritual. Rather, in Pentecost the transcendent and the immanent co-inhere, inviting human participation and improvisation. In the space of this divine-human synergy, the pneumatic imagination is freed to join with the Creator Spirit in remaking the world. The polyrhythmic structures of Pentecost blend into cosmic harmony, reworking established materials to form new songs and new tongues. In doing so, dimensions of the mystery of salvation that have been hidden away are freed to come into the light.

Pentecost as Otherness

One of the least explored aspects of Pentecost is the festival's power of deconstruction: "The dove descending breaks the air / With flame of incandescent terror." Pentecost offers what T. S. Eliot describes as the "intolerable shirt of flame."[29] It is a via negativa calling for abjection. "Abjection," writes Julia Kristeva, "is a resurrection that has gone through death (of the ego). It is an alchemy that transforms the death drive into a start of life, of new significance."[30]

Theophany is another theological category in which to frame the othering, deconstructive power of Pentecost. Frank Macchia writes, "The New Testament descriptions of both Pentecost and the parousia have been tied to Old Testament theophanies. The final coming of God in the 'day of the Lord' was pictured in the Old Testament as a final theophany accompanied by a disruption of the natural elements as portrayed in previous theophanies such as Sinai."[31] On the day of Pentecost, the apostle Peter connected the manifestations of God's presence with the prophet Joel's description of the final theophany

29. T. S. Eliot, "Little Gidding," in *Four Quartets* (Boston: Houghton Mifflin Harcourt, 1968), 49.

30. Julia Kristeva, *Powers of Horror: An Essay on Abjection*, trans. Leon S. Roudiez (New York: Columbia University Press, 1982), 15.

31. Frank Macchia, "Sighs Too Deep for Words: Toward a Theology of Glossolalia," *Journal of Pentecostal Theology* 1 (1992): 56.

(Acts 2:19–20), in which the presence of blood, fire, and smoke accompany the Lord's coming in judgment.

In the pouring out of the Spirit on all flesh, Pentecost not only suspends social barriers and hierarchies; it also dismantles them. It is Word and Spirit at play, a festival that mocks the world's "order of things." Even language itself is questioned. Pentecost frees us from the structures of repression that language represents. It offers an eclipse of words that pushes beyond dialectics in a manner that says what cannot be said.[32]

At Pentecost, Word and Spirit, in the prophetic manner of John the Baptist, work in tandem to clear the way for the coming of Christ's kingdom. Recall the words of John in Luke's Gospel: "I baptize you with water; but one who is more powerful than I is coming. . . . He will baptize you with the Holy Spirit and fire. His winnowing fork is in his hand, to clear his threshing floor and to gather the wheat into his granary; but the chaff he will burn with unquenchable fire" (3:16–17).

Emerging from the fires of Pentecost, the newly constituted cosmos is one that, having been slain and resurrected by the Holy Spirit, is able to taste of God's life and participate in the mission of God's economy. It is a participatory cosmos, humbled and empowered to fulfill the mission of God to make all things well.

Like Horeb, the upper room blossoms as it burns. It is the funeral pyre for sin and darkness and, at the same time, a refreshing wind bringing verdant new creation. Eliot captured the essence of Pentecost in his poem "Little Gidding":

> The dove descending breaks the air
> With flame of incandescent terror
> Of which the tongues declare
> The one discharge from sin and error.
> The only hope, or else despair
> Lies in the choice of pyre of pyre—
> To be redeemed from fire by fire.

32. Cheryl Bridges Johns, "From Babel to Pentecost," in *Towards Viable Theological Education*, ed. John Pobee (Geneva: WCC Publications, 1997), 137.

Who then devised the torment? Love.
Love is the unfamiliar Name
Behind the hands that wove
The intolerable shirt of flame
Which human power cannot remove.
We only live, only suspire
Consumed by either fire or fire.[33]

In Pentecost we find the beginning as well as the end. Pentecost portends what Eliot called "A condition of complete simplicity / (Costing not less than everything)," one in which all manner of thing is made well. In this enchanting cosmic festival, the "tongues of flames are in-folded / Into the crowned knot of fire / and the fire and the rose are one."[34]

The wonder of Pentecost is that it opened a door that has not been closed. This festival continues to invite humans into fellowship with the divine life. It continues to pour out divine love upon all flesh. It continues to claim cosmic space. It continues to scandalize this present order of Babel. It is a festival that came and never went.

The scrolls in the hands of the apostles as well as the scrolls over the hands of King Cosmos indicate the importance of Scripture within the context of Pentecost. When framed within Pentecost, the Bible offers the enchanting possibility of serving God's purposes for the healing of all creation. It is able to help lead the cosmos out of darkness into the light of redemption. Pentecost Scripture creates an imaginative, free space where the Torah embraces the Song of Songs.

33. Eliot, "Little Gidding," 49.
34. Eliot, "Little Gidding," 49.

7

Foundations of the Enchanted Text of Holy Scripture

About two hours southwest of Paris is the UNESCO World Heritage site—Notre Dame de Chartres Cathedral. This magnificent structure, completed in 1220, sits on ground that has housed Christian worship dating back to the fourth century. Prior to that time Chartres was a Druid sacred site. The cathedral is built over an ancient well, which is over one hundred feet deep. There are stories of people being thrown to their deaths in this well. One of the most gripping stories is that of Modesta, thrown into the depths of the well by her father when he learned of her conversion to Christianity. Modesta's statue adorns the portal to the cathedral.

Chartres is a masterpiece of what is known as Gothic architecture. Its design signifies the medieval social imaginary of harmony and the sacred cosmology of a multilayered world. Following Augustinian theology, in which the physical world represented the spiritual realm, Chartres is one grand metaphor. It is a world in which every window, every carved image, the walls, and even the stones on the floor are all part of a grand and mysterious story. With the ability to build flying buttresses, the ceilings of these cathedrals could soar, leaving people speechless and filled with wonder.

In the Neoplatonic social imaginary, the light of divine illumination was needed to lead people to see the spiritual reality hidden within a sinful world. Gothic architecture, with its towering ceilings, opened up more space for grand windows and for light to permeate the space where the church worshiped. Natural light thus became an expression of divine light. Chartres is known for its beautiful and elaborate windows, and the cathedral sings with light as its colorful rays dance throughout the building.

In July 1993 the International Roman Catholic–Pentecostal Dialogue met at a convent in Paris. One afternoon we took a break from our discussions and traveled by train to Chartres. At the doors of the massive cathedral our designated tour guide, a Catholic sister, greeted our group. She welcomed us with a brief overview of the history of Chartres, noting how the outer features of the cathedral foreshadowed the ethos that awaited us inside.

I was drawn to our tour guide, whose face radiated with joy as well as love for the cathedral. It seemed that she and Chartres were a dynamic Spirit-filled synergy. Once inside, our guide showed us the massive rose window and the large labyrinth on the floor. As we progressed toward the nave, the central part of the cathedral, we stopped for a lesson on one of the windows. Our guide instructed us on how to read the Gospel story depicted in the window—from left to right. She then asked us to notice the small image of barrel makers hidden in the right corner of the window. This image signified that this guild had been the sponsors of the window. Their vocation as barrel makers thus became part of the text of Chartres as well as part of the window's larger Gospel story.

Eventually we made our way down the stone steps into the crypt hidden beneath the church. This space, dating from the eleventh century, was the original first floor of the cathedral. As the sister guided our group through the ancient corridors of the crypt, she became more animated. "Look at the faded images on the walls. They depict people who once worshiped here."

At one point the sister led us to a small chapel, where she asked us to sit on the wooden chairs. "Imagine," she said, "what it was like to worship here so many years ago. How close are these people to us today?" Suddenly, she raised her arms and began to worship; a Roman Catholic member of the dialogue, a German New Testament scholar, began to sing in tongues. All of us, Pentecostals and Catholics, joined in the worship. In those sacred moments it seemed that the saints of the past had stepped off the walls and joined us. We were one; we had entered the *mysterium*. It was wonderful; it was life changing.

In the 1790s participants in the French Revolution attempted to destroy Chartres, but a local architect saved the cathedral by cautioning that the rubble from the demolition would clog the city streets. As an alternative, the revolutionaries burned the cathedral's wooden statue of Mary and dedicated Chartres as a "Temple of Reason." The revolution dealt a severe blow to Christianity in France. Most of the priests were either killed or exiled. Enlightenment ideals—*liberté, égalité, fraternité*—replaced the teachings of the church. Yet Chartres continued to stand as a not-so-silent witness to Christianity.

Chartres points to the mysteries of an enchanted world, a "supernatural materialism,"[1] in which the dynamics of the physical and the spiritual realms co-inhere. In the twenty-first century, the cathedral is once again a major pilgrimage site, with the Pentecost pilgrimage being the largest. Each year it draws thousands of pilgrims, who journey by foot from Paris to Chartres. An interesting feature of this pilgrimage is its connection to traditional, "Latin mass" Roman Catholics. Resistance to modernity has come home to Chartres.

Through the years, Enlightenment zealots attempted to make the Bible a temple of reason. However, in recent years we have begun to see a revival of appreciation for the mysterious ethos of Scripture, much like at Chartres. We are realizing that there are multiple

1. James K. A. Smith, *Thinking in Tongues: Pentecostal Contributions to Christian Philosophy* (Grand Rapids: Eerdmans, 2010), 99.

dimensions to the Bible, and each dimension radiates with its own integrity and light. Each room of the biblical text fits into the whole inexhaustible mystery that is Holy Scripture.

Just as Chartres is built on an ancient foundation, the ethos of Scripture stands on ancient ground. Like Chartres, the Bible's design signifies a unified and sacred cosmology, a multilayered world in which every book, every segment, every paragraph, and every sentence has its own integrity, yet each of these is part of the larger story. The Bible not only contains songs but also expresses an ancient harmony: it sings with the light of revelation. Altogether, the various dimensions of the Bible form a dynamic and living synergy.

Travel with me, if you will, down into the most ancient foundation of the Bible. Here I will point out three interconnecting rooms that together form a triadic ontological support system for the enchanted ethos of the Bible: the triune life, Spirit-Word, and revelation.

The Triune Life

The mysterious life of the triune God is the most ancient part of the Bible's ontological foundation. It all begins here. The triune life is a space veiled in mystery, but because of the incarnation of Jesus and the coming of the Spirit, we now have access to its wonders.

The Feast of Pentecost continues to bring God's life to humanity. As the time of his death approached, Jesus made it clear to his disciples that his revelatory presence would not cease on his leaving them. Rather, the revelatory action would be continued by the ongoing presence of the Holy Spirit (John 14:15–31). The disciples would not be left alone. Instead, they would be ushered into the life that was shared by the Father, the Son, and the Spirit. The coming of the Spirit at Pentecost made it possible for Jesus's promises to be fulfilled. A way was made for the followers of Jesus to share in the triune life and to feast at the table of eternal presence. In the words of John Webster, "God's revelation is God's *spiritual* presence."[2]

2. John Webster, *Holy Scripture: A Dogmatic Sketch* (Cambridge: Cambridge University Press, 2003), 14.

In recent decades we've seen a proliferation of theological reflection on the Trinity. In particular, the work of Catherine Mowry LaCugna has been helpful in tracing the history of the relationship between God's being and God's work in restoring creation. Writes LaCugna, "The central theme of trinitarian theology is the relationship between . . . economy and the eternal being of God. The doctrine of the Trinity is the attempt to understand the eternal mystery of God on the basis of what is revealed about God in the economy of redemption. Theology about God is at the same time theology of Christ and the Spirit."[3]

Theological terms denoting the difference between the economy and the eternal being of God are *oikonomia* (God's economy) and *theologia* (God's being). In her research LaCugna traces how, in the separation between *oikonomia* and *theologia*, speculation about the nature of God became abstract and distant from the economy, or mission, of God. She notes that in the earliest centuries (before the First Council of Nicaea), Christian theologians focused on the scriptural revelation of the one God (Father) in the incarnation of the Son and the sending of the Holy Spirit. Their concern was what was disclosed in the economy (*oikonomia*) of God's mysterious plan of salvation.

More recent trinitarian discussions have opened the way for reimaging the ontology of Scripture, placing its purpose in the *oikonomia*. As Webster notes, "Holy Scripture is dogmatically explicated in terms of its role in God's self-communication, that is, the acts of Father, Son, and Spirit which establish and maintain that saving fellowship with humankind in which God makes himself known to us and by us."[4]

The Bible is to be seen in light of the *oikonomia*, and it reveals to humankind the mystery of salvation in Jesus. It makes known the presence of God as well as the plan and purposes of God. This economic vision of the text cannot be disjoined from the actual presence

3. Catherine Mowry LaCugna, *God for Us: The Trinity and the Christian Life* (San Francisco: HarperSanFrancisco, 1991), 22.

4. Webster, *Holy Scripture*, 8.

of the triune God, for God's *oikonomia* and God's nature are married. In other words, the purposes of God manifest in the Bible express the very presence of the Trinity and not merely information about God.

The Holy Spirit makes this intimate knowledge possible. Writes Telford Work, "One begins an account of biblical efficacy with the economic Trinity, and we first meet the economic Trinity in the *person of the Holy Spirit*. Thus, pneumatology is the point of departure for a bibliology."[5]

Grounding Scripture within the economic life of God calls for a christological focus for Scripture, but it also calls for a robust pneumatology. As LaCugna observes, "The life of God—precisely because God is triune—does not belong to God alone. God, who dwells in inaccessible light and eternal glory, comes to us in the face of Christ and the activity of the Holy Spirit."[6] For Webster, the ontology of Scripture is "defined out of the formative economy of the Spirit of God."[7]

Work builds on Barth's christological focus of Scripture but calls for "unsubordinating the Spirit," allowing for a Spirit-Christology of Scripture. Work notes how the bibliologies of Athanasius, Augustine, Barth, and Balthasar "are deeply informed by the particulars of their doctrines of the Trinity."[8] These doctrines heavily emphasize a Christology of the Alexandrian school.

Work juxtaposes the Alexandrian school of christological thought with that of the Antioch school. He declares that "the 'Word-man' Christology of Antioch can be seen in its modern counterpart in Spirit-Christology." The Antioch tradition emphasized not only the humanity but also the work of the Spirit in the ministry of Jesus. Writes Work, "Antioch rightly sensed a profound importance in the Spirit's descent upon Jesus at his baptism." In Work's estimation, "the spirit of Antioch has been reviving."[9]

5. Telford Work, *Living and Active: Scripture in the Economy of Salvation* (Grand Rapids: Eerdmans, 2002), 33.

6. LaCugna, *God for Us*, 1.

7. Webster, *Holy Scripture*, 28.

8. Work, *Living and Active*, 110.

9. Work, *Living and Active*, 111.

Medieval cathedrals such as Chartres were built upon the Alexandrian vision of the world. In their grand design, the mystery of the incarnation is revealed, yet hidden. But, like Chartres, these buildings contain space that speaks of another social imaginary: the school of Antioch. On the walls of these ancient rooms, we see *human space.* Our eyes are not drawn into a vast transcendent heaven; instead, we are invited into a community of women and men.

If we look carefully, we can see *pneumatic space*, reflecting a Spirit-Christology. The people depicted in the art on the walls are worshiping with raised hands, indicating that the liturgy—the enactment of the divine drama—is happening among the people of God. The strange irony is that in the darker space, the one before the flying buttresses, the radiant presence of Christ seems to have been manifested in ecstatic worship in tune with the ecstatic life of God.

I see Hans Boersma's sacramental bibliology reflecting the beautiful Neoplatonic mystery of Chartres. In this vision, much like a grand cathedral, Scripture offers a transcendent, hidden, but *real presence.* While I appreciate this sacramental ontology of Scripture, with all its beauty and metaphors, I want to go deeper—into the crypt, where there is another layer of *real presence.*

The renewed emphasis on Spirit-Christology respects the uniqueness of Jesus as the incarnate Word; at the same time this emphasis gives more trinitarian depth not only to the incarnation but also to the ontology of Scripture. Just as the Spirit was active in the mission of Jesus, the Spirit plays a more active role in the mission of the written Word.

During our time of ecumenical worship in the crypt at Chartres, we understood that the space we inhabited was not the French Revolution's version of a Temple of Reason. Rather, it was a space wherein we were ushered to a table of divine-human fellowship. Here, for a few moments in time, we tasted the glory of sitting together in heavenly places with Christ Jesus (Eph. 2:6). The Bible is our Spirit-filled ethos and guide into the joys of the divine life. It is time to remove any of our idols to the Enlightenment Temple to Reason and experience Pentecost.

The Bible as Spirit-Word

Another ancient part of the foundation of Scripture is Spirit-Word. Given the nature of Scripture as grounded in the triune life, it is proper to identify Spirit-Word as a basic ontological category for the Bible. A Spirit-Christology offers insight here. Just as the Spirit was active and present in the ministry of the incarnate Word, so is the Spirit active and present in the inscripturated Word. In recent centuries too little has been made of the Spirit's role in both Christology and Scripture. Work explains that this reduction of the Spirit can be traced to an overreaction to christological adoptionism, wherein the "Son's sonship was mistakenly perceived to have begun at some point in his earthly life through the coming of the Holy Spirit."[10] The counterreaction led to a stress on the Son's sonship and the Spirit's role as proceeding from the Father and the Son. This stress minimized the role for the Holy Spirit, including reducing the Spirit's work in Scripture to that of witness.

A renewed "Spirit-Christology has helped recover the relevance of the Holy Spirit as the One who conceives, anoints, and empowers Jesus' work in the created order, not just the One who points to it and carries it on in Jesus' absence." The presence of divine Word existed fully in Jesus, and he is present whenever "the biblical message is delivered in the power of the Spirit (cf. 1 Thess. 1:4; 1 Cor. 5:3)."[11]

Thomas F. Torrance points out that in the Old Testament the Hebrew word *ruach* (spirit) differs from the Greek word *pneuma* in that *ruach* conveys an active and concrete presence. Thus to speak of the holy (*qadosh*) spirit in a Hebrew context is to link the transcendent God with the active concreteness of *ruach*. This linking gives expression to the co-inherence of immanence and transcendence. The New Testament carries this idea forward, linking the Spirit with Jesus as the Word of God incarnate.[12]

10. Work, *Living and Active*, 111.
11. Work, *Living and Active*, 113.
12. See Thomas F. Torrance, *Trinitarian Faith: The Evangelical Theology of the Ancient Catholic Church* (London: T&T Clark, 2004).

Writes James Smart, "The Word and the Spirit are inseparable, which is just another way of saying that the Word of God is not a series of words, ideas, beliefs, or propositions, but is God himself in his chosen way of coming to man, and no one has heard God's Word until, in the hearing of the Word, he has received God himself in his Spirit to be the sovereign center of his existence and the wellspring of his life."[13]

Pentecost is an event that, through the pouring out of the Spirit, ushers the Word into the hearts of believers. It is the fulfillment of Jesus's promise to return to his disciples. This ecstatic outpouring of God's presence is bringing about the new creation inaugurated in the resurrection of Jesus. In the Pentecost icon, the image of Cosmos moving out of the darkness, carrying the scrolls containing the writings of the apostles, conveys the uniting of Spirit, Word, and material world. In Pentecost's pneumatic cosmos, there is hope for a new creation.

Scripture, framed within the fires of Pentecost, exists in service of God's mission in Christ to restore creation. In the words of N. T. Wright, "The written word, expressing and embodying the living word of the primitive gospel, was the Spirit-empowered agent through which the one creator God was reclaiming the cosmos, and as such it offered the way to a truly human life."[14] Building on Wright's notion of the written word as "Spirit-empowered agent," more can be said about the Bible's role in human life:

> As Spirit-Word, the Bible is capacitated for this high calling. The same Spirit who filled the incarnate Word fills the written Word. Just as Jesus did not minister apart from the work of the Spirit, the Bible does not speak apart from the work of the Spirit. Just as the Spirit's descent upon Jesus at his baptism was significant, the Spirit's descent on the Day of Pentecost was significant. The Bible does not have the same ontological status as the incarnate Word. It is not divine, but Scripture has its own genuine reality, one that is fit to enter into the divine service.[15]

13. James Smart, *The Strange Silence of the Bible in the Church: A Study in Hermeneutics* (Philadelphia: Westminster, 1970), 100.

14. N. T. Wright, *The Last Word: How to Read the Bible Today* (San Francisco: HarperCollins, 2013), 67.

15. Cheryl Bridges Johns, "Transcripts of the Trinity: Reading the Bible in the Presence of God," *Ex Auditu* 30 (2014): 161. See also Cheryl Bridges Johns, "Grieving,

The divorce between Spirit and Word is costly. When Word is elevated above Spirit, the result is a rigid foundationalist interpretation of Scripture in which "Word" is collapsed into "text." It is an irony that "Bible-believing" churches and scholars, in failing to acknowledge the Spirit's sovereignty, actually dishonor the sovereignty of the Word. As a result, the Bible's voice is distorted, and the very community that seeks to honor that voice distorts it.

When Spirit is elevated above Word, the result is often a reading of the Bible that collapses Spirit into experience, leaving an interpretation of Scripture that veers far from its original intent. In his reflection on the slippery role of experience, Wright notes, "If 'experience' is itself *source* of authority, we can no longer be *addressed* by a word which comes from beyond ourselves. At this point, theology and Christian living cease to be rooted in God himself, and are rooted instead in our own selves."[16]

The tension between Spirit and Word is related to the larger discussions around canon and charisma. Walter Brueggemann notes the "delicate and difficult balance" between canon and charisma, which rejects, on the one hand, a "God-less Torah (legalism)" and, on the other, a "Torah-less God (romanticism)."[17] In dialogue with Brueggemann, Rickie Moore writes, "I would suggest the tension be posed in terms of a Spirit-less Word (rationalism), on the one hand, and a Word-less Spirit (subjectivism), on the other."[18]

Throughout history, we can see glimpses of the unity of Spirit and Word in renewal movements. This unity may last for a while, but eventually the dialectical tension is resolved, one way or another. More

Brooding, Transforming: The Spirit, the Bible, and Gender," in *Grieving, Brooding, and Transforming: The Spirit, the Bible, and Gender*, ed. Cheryl Bridges Johns and Lisa P. Stephenson, Journal of Pentecostal Theology Supplement Series (Leiden: Brill, 2021): 13.

16. N. T. Wright, *Scripture and the Authority of God: How to Read the Bible Today* (New York: HarperCollins, 2011), 102.

17. Walter Brueggemann, *The Creative Word: Canon as a Model for Biblical Education* (Philadelphia: Fortress, 1982), 113–17.

18. Rickie Moore, "Canon and Charisma in the Book of Deuteronomy," in *Pentecostal Hermeneutics: A Reader*, ed. Lee Roy Martin (Leiden: Brill, 2013), 29–30.

recently, Pentecostal and Charismatic movements are making the choice between Spirit and Word. In the face of rapid cultural change and the resulting fear, traditional Pentecostals are giving up their marriage of Spirit and Word in favor of what appears to be safer—namely, fundamentalism's "plain reading of the text." Corresponding to this direction, there has been a decrease of emphasis on prophecy and the gifts of the Spirit. Many Pentecostal churches now have the same forms of worship and study of the Bible as their non-Pentecostal counterparts.

Other Pentecostals and Charismatics are following the path of placing a heavy emphasis on spiritual gifts, but with little regard for Scripture, unless it is used to support the latest prophecy. In these situations, experience (under the guise of Spirit) triumphs over Word, creating chaos and false prophecies.

The same dichotomizing split between Spirit and Word can be seen in Protestantism. Conservatives are emphasizing the Word, especially as it supports traditional orthodoxy in regard to human sexuality. In doing so, they are finding cobelligerents within Evangelicalism and fundamentalism. Liberals emphasize experience and Spirit as the agents revealing new insight into issues of gender and human sexuality. Often, however, the Spirit is collapsed into experience.

In her assessment of the "Great Emergence" taking place in Western Christianity, Phyllis Tickle projects that experience plays a primary role in interpreting Scripture. Writes Tickle, "Pentecostalism . . . offered the Great Emergence its first, solid applied answer to the question of where now is our authority." She wrongly assumes that, for Pentecostals, the "ultimate authority is experiential rather than canonical."[19] While some Pentecostals may put experience over canon, most see the Scriptures as final authority. In addition, the role of the Holy Spirit in both personal and communal Bible study normally takes precedence over experience, and while we know the Holy Spirit through experience, the Holy Spirit cannot be collapsed into experience.

19. Phyllis Tickle, *The Great Emergence: How Christianity Is Changing and Why* (Grand Rapids: Baker Books, 2008), 85.

Ann Monroe's study of the use of the Bible within American Christianity notes that for liberals, the Bible is "a lot like a Rorschach test,"[20] something that reflects a reader's own vision of the world. Monroe concludes that many liberals "read the Bible" as a mirror of their own reflection, such that the Bible as Scripture is no longer there. The Bible is thus remade into a one-way conversation, with the voice of God being cut out.[21]

Scripture finds its life in the Word of God, but Word is more than Scripture. The Word of God is an active subject, bringing the presence and power of the eternal *Logos*. Genesis describes all things coming to be by God speaking them into existence. The Genesis description of Word conveys creative power, a power that brings order out of chaos and light out of darkness.

Genesis gives an account of creation in which the *ruach* (spirit) of God hovers over the waters and in which the words of God speak creation into existence; since the beginning, Word and Spirit have been active in the economy of God. John 1:1–3 identifies this primordial Word: "In the beginning was the Word, and the Word was with God, and the Word was God. He was in the beginning with God. All things came into being through him, and without him not one thing came into being."

Psalm 33 rehashes the creative, life-giving power of the Word. "By the word of the Lord the heavens were made, / and all their host by the breath of his mouth" (v. 6). William M. Wright and Francis Martin draw together the Genesis and Psalm texts: "Like the creation account in Genesis 1, Psalm 33 depicts God effortlessly creating the world by his Word, a simple and powerful fiat that instantiates his will."[22]

The Word of God not only expresses the power of God; it also conveys the presence of God. In fact, there is no such thing as Word without

20. Ann Monroe, *The Word: Imagining the Gospel in Modern America* (Louisville: Westminster John Knox, 2000), 99.

21. Monroe, *Word*, 100–101.

22. William M. Wright IV and Francis Martin, *Encountering the Living God in Scripture: Theological and Philosophical Principles for Interpretation* (Grand Rapids: Baker Academic, 2019), 16.

presence. The Hebrew *dabar* is not an impersonal "word"; it is always deeply personal and relational. For that reason, in the writings of the Old Testament, a person's word was an expression of their identity. Their actions were to convey their word, to the extent that oaths were viewed as legally binding. Likewise, God's Word was an expression of God's being and his faithfulness to that essence of himself. God would not act contrary to his *dabar*. Furthermore, God's presence was an integral part of God's Word. God's Word was not exterior to God's being.

A Pentecost ontology of Scripture does not exclude the Old Testament witness to Spirit-Word; rather, it fulfills it. God's promise to put his Torah (his Word) in humanity and write his law on our hearts (Jer. 31:33) was a promise of God's presence dwelling within us and not merely a promise of inscription of a code of law. It was a promise fulfilled in the life, death, and resurrection of Jesus, the incarnate Word. Furthermore, at Pentecost the power of both the preincarnate Word and the incarnate Word comes to dwell in human hearts. In this coming, Word, Spirit, and flesh found a promised and longed-for unity.

Framed within the power of Pentecost, Scripture's relationship to Spirit-Word is one in which God's power and presence is conveyed through the biblical text. The Bible is not the totality of Word; yet, by the Holy Spirit, Scripture serves as an agent of God, transcribing his life into human hearts. The deeper we go into Scripture, the more we are able to radiate the life of God. We are ordained to be what Charles Wesley called a "transcript of the Trinity."

> Father, Son, and Spirit hear
> Faith's effectual, fervent prayer,
> Hear, and our petitions seal;
> Let us now the answer feel.
> Mystically one with Thee,
> Transcript of the Trinity,
> Thee, let all our nature own
> One in Three, and Three in One.[23]

23. Charles Wesley, "The Communion of the Saints," part 1, in *The Poetical Works of John and Charles Wesley*, vol. 3, *Hymns and Sacred Poems* (London: Printed by William Strahan, 1739), 86.

Revelation

The divorce of Word and Spirit has created all sorts of problems. It is a rift that has contributed to what Webster calls a "disorderly ontology, an isolation of the Bible from its place in God's revelatory activity and from its reception in the community of faith."[24] This separation has given space to the extremes of rigid fundamentalism and chaotic individualism. To heal the rift, it is important to understand the nature and purpose of Scripture within the framework of revelation and the economy of God's communicative grace.

Webster notes that in modernity, revelation is understood in a "dogmatically minimalistic way. . . . Language about revelation became a way of talking, not about the life-giving and loving presence of the God and Father of our Lord Jesus Christ in the Spirit's power among the worshiping and witnessing assembly, but instead of an arcane process of causality whereby persons acquire knowledge through opaque, non-rational operations." Furthermore, the lack of adequate attention to revelation "left the doctrine pitifully weak, . . . scarcely able to extricate itself from the web of objections in which it was entangled."[25] This doctrine of revelation creates a weak ontology of the Bible.

There is the tendency among Evangelicals to collapse revelation into Scripture, thereby reducing both the power of revelation and the power of Scripture. Webster defines this belief as one in which "Scripture precedes and warrants all other Christian doctrine as the formal principle from which those other doctrines are deduced."[26] It is a disenchanted view of revelation, one that fits comfortably into the modern ethos.

The meaning of the inspiration of Scripture needs to be framed within the context of revelation. Writes Webster, "Theological talk of the inspiration of Scripture needs to be strictly subordinate to and dependent upon the broader concept of revelation."[27] Not only

24. Webster, *Holy Scripture*, 6.
25. Webster, *Holy Scripture*, 12.
26. Webster, *Holy Scripture*, 13.
27. Webster, *Holy Scripture*, 31.

do Evangelicals collapse revelation into Scripture but they also have the tendency to collapse revelation into inspiration. When this happens, the Bible is objectified and viewed as "an inspired *product*,"[28] set apart from its source—the divine presence. It is a vision of the Bible that fits nicely into the category of a historical artifact, one that is set apart from the life of God as well as the life of the church. It is *nuda scriptura* (Scripture is the *only rule* of faith) and not *sola scriptura* (Scripture *alone is infallible*).

When seen in the context of revelation, inspiration "is a mode of the Spirit's freedom, not its inhibition by the letter."[29] In this vision of inspiration, the writers of the biblical text are those who yielded to the Spirit's revelation. Those who were "moved by the Holy Spirit spoke from God" (2 Pet. 1:21). Likewise, this vision of inspiration relates to readers as those who maintain the posture of yielding to the Spirit's revelation in Scripture. The process of writing and reading is thus an active response to God's self-manifestation.

Revelation is not merely a past event that can be reviewed, studied, and celebrated. Rather, it is an ongoing expression of God's presence as well as the outworking of God's plan for the new creation. Writes Webster, "God's revelation is God's *spiritual* presence: God is the personal subject of the act of revelation, and therefore revelation can in no way be commodified."[30] God's revelation is the enchanting, divine presence: singing, speaking, acting, and creating. It overcomes all opposition and darkness. It is ancient yet, at the same time, "new every morning" (Lam. 3:23).

In its participation in the restoration and fulfillment of the new creation, the Bible is more than *logos*-word; it is also ethos. The word *ethos* originally meant "stall" or "dwelling." The ethos of Scripture is that of God's presence and fellowship with humanity. This ethos is a deeply moral one, the creation of a *saving fellowship*. Writes

28. Webster, *Holy Scripture*, 33.
29. Webster, *Holy Scripture*, 33.
30. Webster, *Holy Scripture*, 14–15.

William Schweiker, "Ethos suggests a moral ontology, that is, an account of the meaning of our being in the world and how to orient ourselves in the world."[31]

In the context of Pentecost, the ethos of Scripture reflects the moral ontology of relationship. It makes the Bible more than a compilation of rules and principles and calls for participation with revelation in a manner that unites being, knowing, and doing. Writes Work, "*Ethos* names the entire range of characteristics that describe how one lives. . . . The question of biblical authority is ultimately a matter of Scripture's participation in God's character, ultimately a question of its divine ontology."[32]

Participation is thus an important element of revelation. In his *ressourcement* project, Boersma uses participation as the key to weaving a sacramental tapestry uniting the supernatural and the natural.[33] He grounds this vision of participation in the christological focus of the Alexandrian school. For Boersma, the Scriptures contain the sacramental presence of Christ, but due to Neoplatonic metaphysics, it is an indirect presence. For this reason, allegorical interpretation was utilized by many of the church fathers to reveal Christ, who, in the words of Origen, is "hidden like a treasure" (*thesaurus absconditus*) in the Law and the Prophets.[34]

Without a robust Spirit-Christology, participation is limited to the flavor of indirect, contemplative vision. Things are more often hidden than revealed, and there is always the nagging problem of distance. The mystery of Christ, the *mysterium*, is cut off from the work of the Spirit, the "One who conceives, anoints, and empowers

31. William Schweiker, *Responsibility and Christian Ethics* (Cambridge: Cambridge University Press, 1995), 38.

32. Work, *Living and Active*, 63.

33. See Hans Boersma, *Heavenly Participation: The Weaving of a Sacramental Tapestry* (Grand Rapids: Eerdmans, 2011); Boersma, *Scripture as Real Presence: Sacramental Exegesis in the Early Church* (Grand Rapids: Baker Academic, 2017).

34. Origen, *In Canticum canticorum* 1.2, in *Origen: The Song of Songs Commentary and Homilies*, trans. R. P. Lawson, Ancient Christian Writers 26 (New York: Newman, 1957), 69, as quoted in Boersma, *Scripture as Real Presence*, 278.

Jesus' work in the created order, not just the One who points to it and carries it on in Jesus' absence."[35]

Apart from a vibrant pneumatology, the sacramental effects of Scripture reflect the Greek epistemological flavor of *ginōskō* over against the Hebrew *yada*.[36] *Ginōskō* involves distance and requires standing back from something in order to objectively "know" it. It is an indirect, spectator form of knowledge. In contrast, *yada* is knowledge that comes through experience. (*Yada* was sometimes used as a euphemism for lovemaking.) Thomas Groome describes *yada* as a knowing "more by the heart than by the mind, knowing that arises . . . from active and intentional engagement in lived experience."[37]

In comparing *ginōskō* to *yada*, Rudolf Bultmann states, "The OT usage is much broader than the Greek, and the element of objective verification is less prominent than that of detecting or feeling or learning by experience."[38] Spirit-Christology creates the possibility of a direct, and sometimes overwhelming, encounter with the Jesus who continues to save, heal, and deliver.

Under the umbrella of Pentecost, revelation is both profoundly mysterious and deeply experiential. It is an invitation to participate in the joys of the triune life. Writes Webster, "Revelation is a mystery, a making known of the 'mystery of God's will' (Ephesians 1:9). Revelation is the manifest presence of God which can only be held on its own terms, and which cannot be converted into something plain and available for classification. As the gracious presence of God, revelation is itself the establishment of fellowship."[39] Here is

35. Work, *Living and Active*, 111.

36. See Jackie David Johns and Cheryl Bridges Johns, "Yielding to the Spirit: A Pentecostal Approach to Group Bible Study," *Journal of Pentecostal Theology* 1 (1992): 109–34.

37. Thomas Groome, *Christian Religious Education: Sharing Our Story and Vision* (New York: Harper & Row, 1981), 141.

38. Rudolf Bultmann, "γινώσκω, κτλ" [*ginōskō*, etc.], in *Theological Dictionary of the New Testament*, ed. G. Kittel and G. Friedrich, trans. G. Bromiley (Grand Rapids: Eerdmans, 1964), 1:689–719.

39. Webster, *Holy Scripture*, 15.

where participation becomes the fellowship of divine love, a deeply interpersonal encounter.

The term *participation* is not uncommon in the current Age of Authenticity. Recall how both Burning Man and *Sleep No More* (see chap. 3) are sought out because they each offer a high degree of participation. Yet in the Age of Authenticity, participation is limited by the buffered self, which prevents any sense of comingling with the transcendent. Furthermore, participation in the Age of Authenticity is highly individualized, with people on a quest to find their own experience. Shared life, deep fellowship (*koinōnia*), especially with the transcendent realm, is unimaginable. The good news is that the revelatory power of Pentecost shatters the buffered self, making way for a level of existence that does not seem possible in today's world. As Spirit-Word, Scripture possesses a unique power of participation. It serves as a means of uniting the ecstatic life of God with fragile human flesh. "But we have this treasure in clay jars, so that it may be made clear that this extraordinary power belongs to God and does not come from us" (2 Cor. 4:7).

Webster understands that Scripture's work in divine service is achieved in the sanctification of the text. "As the Holy Spirit's work, sanctification is a process in which, in the limitless freedom of God, the creaturely element is given its own genuine reality as it is commanded and moulded to enter into the divine service. . . . Sanctification is making holy."[40]

Not only is Scripture itself made holy and fit for divine service but it also serves as an agent of sanctification. It is the means whereby God's sanctifying grace "targets the distance created between an utterly holy God and all the profanities of human life in order to bridge this gap and enable the church and its Scripture to practice ways of serving God in the world."[41] As Spirit-Word, Scripture continues the revelatory work of healing and sanctifying creation.

40. Webster, *Holy Scripture*, 27.

41. Daniel Castelo and Robert W. Wall, *The Marks of Scripture: Rethinking the Nature of the Bible* (Grand Rapids: Baker Academic, 2019), 79.

At times, revelation comes as the sheer excess of gift, an outpouring of divine presence so overwhelming that humans experience what Pentecostal theologian Steven Land describes as "the intensification of joy."[42] Exuberant joy is most profoundly seen within the liturgy among the dispossessed: dance, laughter, and shouting. Such expressions are often misunderstood as means of escape, but they are far more than that. They are both celebrations of life and defiant protests against cultures of death.

The intensification of joy brought about by divine revelation does not erase human pathos; it enlarges to include the "intensification of sorrow or longing."[43] Tears are often comingled with laughter as persons long for the not-yet to be realized in the world. When the not-yet of human pathos is taken into the pathos of God, then people, in tandem with the Holy Spirit, groan with sighs "too deep for words" (Rom. 8:22–26). The pathos of God is deep and wide. It encompasses all brokenness. The mystery of the incarnation—the birth, life, death, and resurrection of Jesus—guarantees the restoration of all things. This mystery holds together the tension between the already and the not-yet. The Holy Spirit—as "the first fruits" (8:23), sign, and seal of the mystery of salvation (cf. 2 Cor. 1:22; Eph. 1:13; 4:30)—broods over the chaos (Gen. 1:2), calling it with longing into restoration.

Within the grand canopy of Pentecost, there is continuity between the filling of human flesh, human flesh yielding to the Spirit in the writing of sacred Scripture, and human flesh preserving and teaching the Scripture. The Bible as a divine-human document is thus a sanctified, Spirit-filled, missional text capable of guiding King Cosmos out of darkness and into the light of God's new creation.

The canonization of Scripture can be seen as corporate discernment of the Spirit's freedom and not merely recognition of the letter. As a communion in the Holy Spirit, the church's role in canonization is one of active participation in God's revelation of his plan and

42. Steven J. Land, *Pentecostal Spirituality: A Passion for the Kingdom* (Sheffield: Sheffield Academic, 2001), 99.

43. Land, *Pentecostal Spirituality*, 99.

purposes. A Pentecost church allows for revelation to weave a seamless garment of Word, Spirit, and community.

Full Circle: Sacred Space and Pilgrimage

In the fall of 2016 I visited Igreja Pentecostal Deus é Amor, along with a retired Methodist bishop and two academic colleagues. The large church sits in a poor area of Sao Paulo, Brazil. As we were driving up to the building, I noticed that outside the temple were booths where vendors cooked and sold food. A homeless encampment sat across the street from the church. People were milling around the church as well as going into and coming out of the building. The church and its outside perimeter served as a liminal space where the lines between the outside world of poverty and the inner world of the temple were fluid.

At the doors of the temple a woman wearing a pink dress, the standard attire for women deacons, greeted us. She took us on a tour of the building, one that had a central sanctuary for large worship gatherings as well as many side rooms that were regularly used for worship, prayer, and Bible study. One room in particular was set aside for intercessory prayer. More women wearing pink dresses monitored the room. The atmosphere of this room was charged and filled with the sounds of fervent prayer. In this sacred space, the chaos from the outside world was invited into sacred Presence. Here, under the guidance of powerful deacons, the chaos was invited into the sacred circle where it was overcome. Sometimes these prayers took hours, but there was no hurry. Serious work called for groaning, intercessory prayer.

Waldo Cesar, in his description of temples among the Brazilian poor, noted that the "dimensions of this internal space favor extensive movement inside the churches—a covered pilgrimage" in which there are "several bridges or networks that are momentarily established in these physical acts of walking, kneeling, placing their hands on the head of the person beside them, crying with him or her, laughing at oneself, and leaving with a new hope of life."[44]

44. Richard Shaull and Waldo Cesar, *Pentecostalism and the Future of the Christian Churches* (Grand Rapids: Eerdmans, 2000), 68–69.

The poor leave their sacred space with "another vision of the world, an alternate, unconventional way of facing poverty, illness, unemployment, violence."[45] Their unconventional pilgrimage in a sacred space, where they are not rejected, turns into another pilgrimage into the external space where, even though oppressed and rejected, they are bearers of the Word.

There are many differences between this temple of the poor and Chartres. However, I have discovered that the Spirit-Word inhabits both spaces. In Chartres, this presence is revealed within stained-glass images, in the chants of the choir, in the prayers of the people, in the Eucharist, in the homilies, and in the witness of saints long departed. With its emphasis on the transcendent, hidden truths of the *mystērion*, Chartres is a living expression of the Alexandrian school. Its hospitality fits well with Origen's homily on the three visitors at the Oaks of Mamre. In Origen's allegorical reading of this event, everything is filled with mystery.[46]

In the Brazilian temple, the presence of the Spirit-Word is revealed in the street vendors on the sidewalk; in the homeless camp just outside the doors of the church; among the poor finding hope and healing; in the preaching and teaching of those animated by the Spirit; and among the bodies that, with ecstatic abandon, join the dance of the triune life. Perhaps this temple represents the Antioch school, where the preaching of John Chrysostom would be right at home: straightforward with an emphasis on the radical immanence of God (*synkatabasis*) among the poor and the presence of a robust Spirit-Christology. Chrysostom ends his homily on Abraham's visitors with the words of Jesus: "For I was hungry, and you gave me food, I was thirsty and you gave me something to drink, I was a stranger and you welcomed me, I was sick and you took care of me, I was in prison and you visited me" (Matt. 25:35–36).

45. Shaull and Cesar, *Pentecostalism*, 69.

46. I'm indebted to Hans Boersma's "Hospitable Reading," his chapter in *Scripture as Real Presence*, 56–80, for its insight into the schools of Alexandria (Origen) and Antioch (Chrysostom) and their readings of the account of Abraham's three visitors at Mamre (Gen. 18).

The multidimensional nature of Scripture is a beautiful, Spirit-filled ethos. It invites us to enter the Pentecost mystery built upon the foundations of the triune life, Spirit-Word, and revelation. For some, this space will be along the lines of the Alexandrian sacramental vision, a thin place that invites contemplation. In this setting, Scripture is chanted and sung in celestial harmony, and allegory plumbs the depths of the mystery of the hidden Christ.

For others, sacred scriptural space is more like a temple among the poor, a place where real presence takes on the character of deliverance from oppression and the healing of sick bodies. It's a space where the common people find a hospitable table spread for them and Spirit-Word plays in improvisational form.

8

Dimensions of the Enchanted Text of Holy Scripture

Grand cathedrals are built upon an ancient foundation. Above the hidden foundation exists an enchanted, multidimensional space—windows radiating with light, floors of intricate tile mosaics, altars of sacramental presence, stone carvings of both human and nonhuman beings. Scripture is built upon the foundation of the triune life, Spirit-Word, and revelation. Rising from this deep space, the ethos of Scripture reveals many enchanted dimensions. I name and discuss four: the sacramental dimension, the dimension of communion, the imaginative dimension, and the dimension of Holy Otherness.

The Sacramental Dimension

Walter Brueggemann identifies Scripture as having the power to "redescribe the world."[1] In Pentecost, Scripture has both the power to redescribe the world and the sacramental power to bring about the real presence of that world. This world is a meetinghouse, a space for the risen incarnate Word to dwell with his people.

1. Walter Brueggemann, *The Word That Redescribes the World: The Bible and Discipleship* (Minneapolis: Fortress, 2006).

The sacramental dimensions of the biblical text can be described as a place in which "the transcendent inheres in immanence," according to James K. A. Smith.[2] As I have written elsewhere, "In the power of Spirit-Word, the materiality of the biblical text abounds with real presence. It is a space that offers potential for re-orientation of existence; it is transforming space, alive and radiating by the Holy Spirit. Scriptural space offers a truth that seizes and captures us in its holy power."[3]

Utilizing Smith's description of the relationship between nature and the supernatural, we could say that Scripture is "already suspended and inhabited by the Spirit such that it is always *primed* for the Spirit's manifestations." Within the primed nature of Scripture are the dynamics of the Spirit's presence in working with the writers of the text, taking hold of their minds, and uniting them in a divine-human synergy that is rational as well as transrational. Add to these dynamics the presence of the Spirit in those who read and perform the biblical text, taking their minds into the space of divine-human synergy, and grabbing hold of their vocal cords in the text's performance. All these dynamics take up "aspects of creation to manifest the glory of God."[4]

In this sense, the meaning of "sacramental" carries with it dynamics of a presence that is both mysterious and yet starkly real and inviting. In a Pentecostal sacramental vision of the text, the *mystērion* is hidden, waiting to be discovered, even as it is a gift being poured out in sheer excess. In both the discovering and the receiving, humanity is invited to enter the liminal space that is the threshold between the supernatural and natural worlds. "This sacred zone offers to readers what the Russian philosopher Nikolai Berdyaev described as 'the quantitative depth of existential time.' In this dimension, time is drawn as a vertical line as well as a horizontal one. It is a dimension

2. James K. A. Smith, *Thinking in Tongues: Pentecostal Contributions to Christian Philosophy* (Grand Rapids: Eerdmans, 2010), 100.

3. Cheryl Bridges Johns, "Grieving, Brooding, Transforming: The Spirit, the Bible, and Gender," in *Grieving, Brooding, and Transforming: The Spirit, The Bible, and Gender*, ed. Cheryl Bridges Johns and Lisa P. Stephenson, Journal of Pentecostal Theology Supplement Series 46 (Leiden: Brill, 2021), 15.

4. Smith, *Thinking in Tongues*, 101.

that may be called 'eschatological time,' for within its realm the eternal breaks into the temporal, and the Bible becomes an icon wherein 'the light from the future streams into the present.'"[5]

Performance of the Bible creates a thin space where the veil between the supernatural and the natural world becomes transparent: by the Spirit we enter into a dimension of time wherein the "past draws near and the future bends toward the present. Reading the text is, therefore, an eschatological experience, a transtemporal journey that brings participants into the eternal presence of God."[6]

Scripture is more than a static and discrete entity. It is an "enspirited" closed canon existing in service of dynamic and ongoing revelation. The power of ongoing revelation allows for the closed canon of Scripture to reveal the ever-active, ever-present life of God. It offers what Smith describes as a "continually 'open' universe, evidenced in the miraculous and God's continued activity in the world."[7]

Within this dynamic system, Scripture's sacramental character is such that it serves as an efficacious sign; it causes to be that to which it points. Clark Pinnock observes, "Pentecostals read the Bible not primarily as a book of concepts, but as a very dynamic activity of ongoing divine activity. They inhabit the story-world of the Bible and experience God according to the pattern narrated by the biblical text." In this sense, Pinnock goes on to say, "Reading the Bible in a Spirit-filled community allows participants to receive biblical metaphors "not as symbols to be transcended but as reality-depicting language."[8]

The Dimension of Communion

Given these Pentecostal sacramental dynamics, the ontology of Scripture is relational to its core. First, it offers the presence of a God who

5. Johns, "Grieving, Brooding, Transforming," 14. See also Nikolai Berdyaev, *Slavery and Freedom* (New York: Scribner's Sons, 1944), 261.

6. Johns, "Grieving, Brooding, Transforming," 14.

7. Smith, *Thinking in Tongues*, 13.

8. Clark Pinnock, "Divine Relationality: A Pentecostal Contribution to the Doctrine of God," *Journal of Pentecostal Theology* 16 (2000): 9.

exists in triune relationality. Second, Scripture opens a path toward what the ante-Nicene church referred to as "union and communion" with God. Third, Scripture offers communion with other believers: past, present, and future.

God's life as relational and personal defines the parameters of Scripture's role in the economic life of God. The end goal of God's mission is restoration of divine-human fellowship. Thus the type of relationship facilitated by Scripture is one of both communion with and personal experience of the triune life. Following the Protestant Christocentric reading of Scripture, Evangelicals place the Bible in service of leading people to experience a deeper, personal relationship with Jesus. This view of the Bible leaves little room for the expansive fullness of a relationship with Jesus existing in trinitarian communion. Often the Holy Spirit is marginalized to the role of a nonintrusive agent guiding people in personal Bible study. In this model, the presence of the Spirit is secondary to the power of the human subject. The presence of the Father is remotely transcendent.

In a Spirit-Word vision of the text, performance of the Bible creates a space for the presence of Jesus existing in trinitarian communion. Thus the mission of Scripture, in the words of Telford Work, is to participate "in the will of the Father, in the *kenōsis* of the Son, and [in] the power of the Holy Spirit."[9] This vision of Scripture necessitates that human readers see themselves as entering into a relational, trinitarian world and not a private room with a sign on the door reading "Me and Jesus."

In his work on ante-Nicene catechesis, Jackie Johns points out that the Holy Spirit served as the dynamic *pedagogue*, bringing believers into union and communion with God. "The ultimate goal of union with God was two faceted," writes Johns. "First, in a very real sense union with God was attainable in the present life through the communion of the Holy Spirit. . . . Second, union with God was yet to be fully realized. The believer's experience of the Spirit was considered

9. Telford Work, *Living and Active: Scripture in the Economy of Salvation* (Grand Rapids: Eerdmans, 2002), 170.

preparatory for a future and a final union with God."[10] Johns notes a third pedagogical role of the Spirit: "the preparation of believers for their final union with God through their salubrious union with the body of Christ. . . . Specifically, the *charismata*, or gifts of the Spirit, were administered of the Spirit, were administered through various individuals for the good of others (1 Cor. 12:12–31)."[11]

Within a pneumatically configured framework, Scripture has a centripetal force; it pulls people into union and communion with the divine life and into unity with fellow believers. Scripture offers a joining of Spirit, Word, and community. Interpretation of Scripture takes place in the framework of this triadic joining. "The dialectical relationship between Spirit and Word," writes Amos Yong, "is played out in the context of Community. The dialectical relationship between Spirit and Community is anchored in Word. Spirit implicates Word and Community; Word implicates Spirit and Community; Community implicates Word and Spirit."[12]

The Imaginative Dimension

The imaginative dimension of Scripture works to tear down barriers the modern world has constructed: logic versus imagination, reason versus emotion, and natural versus supernatural. It works to remix the realms of transcendence and immanence. The Holy Spirit, the great master of the imagination, is present as our guide in this dimension. Eugene Peterson writes, "The great masters of the imagination

10. Jackie Johns, *The Pedagogy of the Holy Spirit according to Early Christian Tradition* (Cleveland, TN: Center for Pentecostal Ministries, 2012), 76–77. Johns references Irenaeus: "Jesus 'has poured out the Spirit of the Father for the union and communion of God and man, imparting indeed God to men by means of the Spirit, and, on the other hand, attaching man to God by His own incarnation, and bestowing upon us at His coming immortality durably and truly, by means of communion with God.'" Johns, *Pedagogy of the Holy Spirit*, 74, quoting Irenaeus, *Against Heresies* 5.1.1, in *Ante-Nicene Fathers* 1:527.

11. Johns, *Pedagogy of the Holy Spirit*, 78.

12. Amos Yong, *Spirit-Word-Community: Theological Hermeneutics in Trinitarian Perspective* (Eugene OR: Wipf & Stock, 2002), 18.

do not make things up out of thin air; they direct our attention to what is right before our eyes. They train us to see it whole—not in fragments but in context, with all the connections. They connect the visible with the invisible, the *this* with the *that*."[13] The Spirit helps us see what is right before our eyes and to see things whole.

Scripture is a place where the pneumatic imagination flourishes. The Spirit's work in the writing, canonization, and transmission of Scripture is not unlike the Spirit's work in creation: it brings together the Word and the material world. Just as the natural world is a masterpiece of creative imagination, so too is scriptural space. Through Scripture, the Spirit creatively employs human imagination in re-scripting the new creation.

In the opening of his letter to the church at Ephesus, Paul gives a beautiful and deep description of God's plan of salvation in Christ Jesus. It is as if Paul stepped inside God's imagination, his grand plan that includes "every spiritual blessing in the heavenly places" (Eph. 1:3); a plan that "chose us in Christ before the foundation of the world" (v. 4); a plan for our "adoption as his children through Jesus Christ" (v. 5); a plan that gives us "redemption, . . . the forgiveness of our trespasses" (v. 7); a plan "for the fullness of time, to gather up all things" (v. 10); a plan for an inheritance (v. 11). Paul notes that on hearing the word of truth, the gospel, believers were "marked with the seal of the promised Holy Spirit; this is the pledge of our inheritance" (vv. 13–14). Paul goes on to remind believers that "God, who is rich in mercy, out of the great love with which he loved us even when we were dead through our trespasses, made us alive together with Christ—by grace you have been saved—and raised us up with him and seated us with him in the heavenly places in Christ Jesus, so that in the ages to come he might show the immeasurable riches of his grace in kindness toward us in Christ Jesus" (2:4–7).

When we read the words of Paul about being seated "in the heavenly places in Christ Jesus" and recognize the mystical and mysterious

13. Eugene Peterson, *Run with the Horses: The Quest for Life at Its Best*, 2nd ed. (Downers Grove, IL: InterVarsity, 2009), 74.

manner of the expression as Spirit-Word, this passage of Scripture serves to take us into those heavenly places and to seat us with Christ Jesus. As readers who are sealed by the Holy Spirit, we are not merely to contemplate what it is like to be sitting in heavenly places with Christ Jesus (although that is certainly part of the process of studying this text); we are also to open ourselves to the reality of being there, for in truth, *we are there.*

It is important to note Paul's prayer for the Ephesians: "I pray that the God of our Lord Jesus Christ, the Father of glory, may give you a spirit of wisdom and revelation . . . so that, with the eyes of your heart enlightened, you may know . . . what are the riches of his glorious inheritance among the saints, and what is the immeasurable greatness of his power for us who believe" (1:17–19). This prayer continues today—we need "a spirit of wisdom and revelation" and the enlightenment of the eyes of our heart—so that we may know whose we are and where we are.

When we realize whose we are and where we are, reading and studying Scripture becomes an act of worship, an experience of fellowship with the triune life. Whenever I am in that space, I find it hard to leave, for I know that in the leaving, some of the enchanted wonder will dissipate. The same Spirit who took Paul into the heavenly places is present, some two thousand years later, to take us on that same journey. In the beautiful, imaginative ethos of Scripture, we are mysteriously joined with Christ, Paul, and all the saints.

Scripture's pneumatic imagination is most profoundly seen at play among the oppressed. In his assessment of the Bible in the majority world, Philip Jenkins describes the reading of a Pauline text in a northern community of Kenya. After the preacher's reading of Paul's blessing for the Corinthian church—"My love be with all of you in Christ Jesus" (1 Cor. 16:24)—the community responded in unison, "Thank you, Paul." Jenkins writes, "Paul might not have been physically present, but he had been kind enough to send his best wishes."[14] The pneumatic and communal imagination of these

14. Philip Jenkins, *The New Faces of Christianity: Believing the Bible in the Global South* (Oxford: Oxford University Press, 2006), 27.

Kenyan Christians includes not only themselves but also the apostle Paul and the company of the Corinthian believers.

In its service of the divine economy, Scripture creates zones of liberation and freedom in which people find themselves joined to stories of others whose desperate lives received healing and deliverance. Thus the Word mediates the biblical realities such that there is "a constant, mutually conditioning interplay between knowledge and lived experience," says Steven Land.[15] In these zones, Rickie Moore writes, "Learning about God and directly experiencing God perpetually inform and depend upon one another."[16]

Within modernity's immanent frame, Bible study fits nicely into Charles Taylor's category of "disciplines of disenchantment." Unaware of our stunted imagination, we work hard to keep away any sense of real presence. (After all, who needs the imagination and real presence to distill truths and principles, and to apply them?) Often, going to a group Bible study is less magical, less imaginative than attending a movie. All too often it is just a gathering of what Smith calls "thinking things," people assuming a disembodied approach to the text.[17] Within this approach, it is easy to assume the hermeneutical arc of theory to application. Normally the biblical passage is read and studied, after which there will be an attempt to make meaning of the passage in life. Sometimes the Holy Spirit is referenced as the agent who helps in application of the text, but the whole process of studying and applying is guided by human reason. The safe, comfortable space of *distance* prevents transcendence from impinging on the immanent frame. With so little acknowledgment of the affective domain, the eyes of the heart remain closed.

In some places of the world, however, the pneumatic imagination stands in the gap between life and death. In these situations, people employ a pneumatic imagination in their reading of the Bible that

15. Steven J. Land, *Pentecostal Spirituality: A Passion for the Kingdom* (Sheffield: Sheffield Academic, 2001), 75.

16. Rickie Moore, "A Pentecostal Approach to Scripture," *Seminary Viewpoint* 8, no. 1 (1987): 1–2.

17. Smith, *Thinking in Tongues*, 60–61.

offers the possibility of what Richard Shaull describes as "reconstruction of life." Many of the world's poor live in "a prison . . . in a sense, on their own 'death row,' facing total deprivation." In their engagement with the Bible, Spirit-Word opens a portal into eschatological space, one in which the "gates of their prison have been unlocked, . . . a world in which the sick are being healed, broken families restored, broken lives put together again, and desperate economic situations often changed."[18] This power of the pneumatic imagination allows for the actualization of the world that the Spirit is seeking to create.

During the eras of slavery, Jim Crow, and segregation, the liberating power of the pneumatic imagination was central to African American readings of the Bible. As James Cone wrote, "Black people needed liberating visions so that they would not let historical limitations determine their perception of black being. . . . The one theme that stood out above all other themes was liberation."[19]

Danté Stewart gives a poignant description of the imaginative power of the Bible in the hands of "Black folk" in the context of a country that still clings to its racism:

> There's an old King James Version Bible sitting on my bookshelf. It is black, rugged; the gold lining on the pages shines as light hits it. The jacket is missing, and the threads have unloosened from one another over the years. It has been tried. It has traveled across the South, across time. Now it sits on a shelf where it keeps the company of books written by Black folk. Black folk who have read a similar Bible, who have wrestled with it, been confused by it. Black folk who have held it as tight as I do today.
>
> When I open up this old Bible, dusty words emerge, conjuring up memories of poetic sermons and sweaty mics smelling like old metal and stank breath. I am suddenly surrounded by preachers and mothers and friends and saints and sinners who tried to love and live

18. Richard Shaull and Waldo Cesar, *Pentecostalism and the Future of the Christian Churches* (Grand Rapids: Eerdmans, 2000), 153.

19. James H. Cone, *God of the Oppressed* (New York: Seabury, 1975), 60–61.

> well—while failing, learning, and trying again. When I read these ancient scriptures, I hear the way they flowed from my momma's lips. What was it about this book that kept her up in the middle of the night, calling on the Lord, calling out our names, calling out things that she imagined possible for all of us? What was it that kept her crying out when the world around her was burning?
>
> When she recited scripture, she spoke it poetically, adding the old *-eth* at the end of words like her King James Version did. Those words carried the divine. It was as transporting as fiction, yet nothing like fiction. Something you could only call magical, yet nothing like magic. The words were an entire world, but they were also in her Black body in this white country. These words carried both weight and worth and worship and worry and whatever "w" words you can describe—words that put you back together again when you, your body, and your country are shattered. . . . Indeed, to hear this language is to hear the voice of God upon us in a land that has never truly known God or Love or Blackness.[20]

Stewart's account of the Bible in the hands of "Black folk" illustrates how the pneumatic imagination blends with the prophetic imagination. The pneumatic Spirit is also the prophetic Spirit, especially when the world being imaginatively scripted clashes with the dominant social imaginary. Writes Walter Brueggemann, "*Prophetic* must be *imaginative* because it is urgently out beyond the ordinary and the reasonable."[21]

The ethos of Scripture invites us to "come and taste" the world being scripted by the Spirit. It is easy to think that the imaginative, Spirit-filled ethos of the Bible is far out of reach, that we are too stunted in our capacity to open the eyes of our heart. I believe that it's not too late and that re-enchantment is possible. Humans are created to inhabit the enchanted world of God. It is our natural home.

20. Danté Stewart, *Shoutin' in the Fire: An American Epistle* (New York: Convergent, 2021), 3–4.

21. Walter Brueggemann, *The Prophetic Imagination*, 40th anniversary ed. (Minneapolis: Fortress, 2018), xxix.

The Dimension of Holy Otherness

In the pneumatically configured space of Scripture, the Paraclete serves as the Divine Pedagogue, leading us into the truth of God, self, and world. The Pentecost unity of Spirit-Word results in the piercing, dividing, and judging of thoughts and intentions. In this dimension, Scripture offers the Protestant principle of freedom of the Word, an outside force that refuses domestication. It is "living and active, sharper than any two-edged sword, piercing until it divides soul from spirit, joints from marrow; it is able to judge the thoughts and intentions of the heart" (Heb. 4:12).

This living and active text refuses domestication. "Not unlike the realm of the Holy of Holies in the temple, the otherness of sacred scriptural territory is both wonderful and dangerous. It is wonderful because in it we find the delights of the Triune life offered to us out of God's ecstatic self-giving. It is dangerous because this space offers to us God as the transcendent, living subject. Here we are known and read more than we know and read."[22]

The holy otherness of Scripture invites us into the wonderment of the world it describes. On these occasions, the Bible opens up before us the beauty of creation, heroic lives of faithful people, poetry, and harmonious music. Most importantly, the Bible reveals Jesus, the Living Word. "He is the image of the invisible God" (Col. 1:15). The Gospel stories of Jesus narrate the presence and power of God made visible. These stories have the capacity to fill us with wonder and amazement. Revelation fills us with both wonder of heavenly worship and the terror of judgment on the empires of this world.

Even as it creates wonder, the otherness of Scripture also offers the possibility of negation. As noted earlier, Julia Kristeva stresses reading as an act of divestment or abjection of something internal to the reader. According to Kristeva, "Abjection is a resurrection that has gone through death (of the ego). It is an alchemy that transforms the death drive into a start of life, of new significance." She understands

22. Johns, "Grieving, Brooding, Transforming," 15.

that abjection of self is "fully assumed by or described in the New Testament, especially in Saint Paul, and in such Christian writers as Saint Augustine, Saint Bernard of Clairvaux, and Saint Thomas Aquinas."[23]

Kristeva's view of the necessity for abjection points to the power of holy otherness. A disenchanted world is one in which the fearful human self-rules. The self can objectify the world, and it asks the objectified world to relinquish its power in service of the self. In such a world, the autonomous self remains protected. A protected self cannot be redeemed.

As a deconstructive force, Scripture provides a continuous reconfiguration of the world, self, and language. Inherent within this dimension exists the Word's powerful gestalt of deconstruction and reconstruction with the ability to tear apart and dismantle as well as to unite and create order. The deconstructive side of Scripture is most frightening and disturbing to the modern mind. Its *via negativa* mocks the modernist belief that humanity can construct a livable habitation by utilizing the skills of rational analysis and problem solving.

A Pentecost text offers the gift of otherness, a presence that disrupts the present with both promise and judgment (re: Peter's sermon on the day of Pentecost and his references to Joel 2:28).[24] Within this framework, Scripture offers the invitation to yield to the Spirit-Word, and thus be exposed and known.

Rickie Moore, in his work on the charismatic dimensions of Deuteronomy, writes, "The charismatic dimension of the book Deuteronomy" contains "an overwhelming encounter with the ultimate 'outside' source." Moore suggests that such a theophanic encounter

23. Julia Kristeva, *Powers of Horror: An Essay on Abjection*, trans. Leon S. Roudiez (New York: Columbia University Press, 1982), 88, 121, as quoted in Wesley Kort, *"Take, Read": Scripture, Textuality, and Cultural Practice* (University Park: Pennsylvania State University Press, 1996), 114–15.

24. For further reflection on the deconstructive power of Pentecost, see Cheryl Bridges Johns, "Meeting God in the Margins: Ministry among Modernity's Refugees," in *The Papers of the Henry Luce III Fellows in Theology*, ed. Matthew Zyniewicz, ATS Series in Theological Scholarship and Research 3 (Atlanta: Scholars Press, 1999), 7–27.

is an "utterly confessional moment," a time of "being claimed," an experience of "utter criticism." These moments expose what it means "to stand stripped down to the nakedness and weakness of one's confessions."[25]

Theophanic encounters expose the impotence of the ordered, technical, and rational world in which modern Christians stake *their claim*. In light of the possibility of *being claimed*, it is easy to yield to the temptation of walling off the possibilities of chaos and to replace the freedom of the Word with rigid order. In doing so, we remove Scripture from its service in the economy of salvation and place our own schemes into the service of protecting *our rights* to make *our claims*.

Writes Andrew Root, "The transcendent mystery is that when negation—elimination of being by some force—is shared by both human and divine persons, it creates the deepest of unions."[26] This is the mystery of the cross. As Christians, we are invited to share in the death of Jesus. In the union of our death and the death of Christ, a space is created where the Spirit moves, turning death into life. The *via negativa* of the cross is the path to life.

You may ask, "How can any human relate to such a text? How can we possibly interpret its meaning? Operating out of a flat, two-dimensional mind of Enlightenment rationalism, we cannot truly know and understand the Bible. A new vision of the text requires a new vision of the readers, one that moves beyond human beings as merely cognitive beings."[27] The good news is that we are created for the enchanted multidimensional, sacred world of the Bible. Just as the Bible is ontologically grounded in the triune life, so is humanity. Just as the Bible may be defined as Spirit-Word, humans may be defined as spirit-flesh. Just as the Bible is sacramental, humans are created to be living icons of the Presence.

25. Rickie D. Moore, "Deuteronomy and the Fire of God: A Critical Charismatic Interpretation," *Journal of Pentecostal Theology* 7 (1995): 22.

26. Andrew Root, *Faith Formation in a Secular Age: Responding to the Church's Obsession with Youthfulness* (Grand Rapids: Baker Academic, 2017), 130.

27. Cheryl Bridges Johns, "Transcripts of the Trinity: Reading the Bible in the Presence of God," *Ex Auditu* 30 (2014): 164.

9

Re-enchanting the People of God

In 1994, I was part of the international Roman Catholic–Pentecostal dialogue taking place at Kappel Monastery, a beautiful location near Zurich, Switzerland. The monastery, now Kappel Abbey, is just down the road from the site of the Second War of Kappel, where Swiss Reformer Ulrich Zwingli was killed in a bloody battle between Protestants and Catholics in 1531. Now, 463 years later, Roman Catholics and Pentecostals gathered here around the theme "Evangelization, Proselytism, and Common Witness." Two years into a round of dialogues that would last seven years, we all had hopes that we could better understand one another's heart for common witness; we desired to quell the ongoing battle for souls that had been waging for decades. It was a battle that could, at times, turn violent.

Cistercian monks built the monastery in 1185. They served the area until it was taken over by the Reformers. Following the Reformation, the site was run by the city of Zurich, which used it as a home for the poor, a school for orphans, and various other projects. In 1983, the Protestant Reformed Church took over the former monastery; now they use it as a retreat center. Today, various groups and church organizations are welcomed to this sacred and beautiful space.

While we were having our dialogue, I noticed some things that appeared out of place in a Christian monastery. Stones and feathers were carefully arranged in the deep windowsills of the ancient building. In the room next to where our group was meeting, some women sat in a circle around burning candles arranged in the shape of a pentagram. In the evenings the women joined in a circle dance on the outside courtyard overlooking a beautiful landscape of open fields.

One afternoon I worked up the nerve to talk with one of the leaders of the women's retreat. She told me she was part of a growing group of people expressing dissatisfaction with the "sterile rationalism" of the Reformed churches. Seeking an embodied and more mysterious faith, some people, such as the women on retreat, were returning to the pre-Christian religion of their ancestors. After our conversation I thought about the Cistercian monks who once lived in this sacred space. It seemed that things had come full circle. What would they say about the Christian mission today?

Those of us meeting in Kappel during a warm July in 1994—Roman Catholics, Pentecostals, neo-pagans—fulfilled B. B. Warfield's warning of the world once again becoming infected with magic and superstition. For Warfield, Roman Catholics were the "old magic." Pentecostals were the "new magic." The neo-pagans were the "very old magic." During that week, Kappel represented a fundamentalist Christian's nightmare!

Reflecting back on this setting, I now see how it was a harbinger of the landscape of religion in the twenty-first century, one where, for the most part, Roman Catholics and Pentecostals are no longer enemies. In fact, they are the two dominant forms of Christianity, often intermingling to the degree that it is hard to tell them apart. Traditional forms of Protestantism continue to decline. A good number of those leaving Protestantism are returning to what Max Weber called "the embrace of the old churches."[1] Ancient liturgies are now

1. Max Weber, "Science as Vocation," in *The Vocation Lectures*, trans. Rodney Livingstone, ed. David Owen and Tracy Strong (Indianapolis: Hackett, 2004), 30.

the new thing. Like the women who left the Reformed Church of Switzerland, some people are turning to forms of neo-paganism to fill their enchantment deficit.

The women on retreat at Kappel knew they were created to be *more*. Deep down they had a hunch that they were somehow designed to be spiritual, embodied beings who could express their faith by dancing in the light of the setting sun or by sitting in a circle, praying and chanting around burning candles. They wanted a faith that joined heaven and earth, body and spirit, mind and matter. They also knew that their current faith and their modern Protestant Bible offered little that would help them find that *more*. After the retreat, they would return to the largely secular immanent frame, where from time to time they could carve out some degree of enchanted space.

In their hunger for re-enchantment, these women were ripe for what may be called "re-evangelization." If the ancient Cistercian monks—the ones who had evangelized the ancestors of these women—could speak, they would advise us to take a more mystical, embodied approach to evangelism. In fact, Bernard of Clairvaux (1090–1153), the founder of their order and the person who had authorized the Kappel mission, was known for his starkly sensual poetry:

> Lord, with my mouth I touch and worship Thee,
> With all the strength I have I cling to Thee,
> With all my love I plunge my heart in Thee,
> My very life-blood would I draw from Thee,
> O Jesus, Jesus I draw me into Thee.[2]

Whatever form evangelization and discipleship takes in the twenty-first century, it must offer the possibility of re-enchantment. Like the women at Kappel, many Western people are longing for something

2. "Rhythmical Prayer to the Sacred Members of Jesus Hanging upon the Cross," ascribed to St. Bernard, trans. Emily Mary Shapcote, in St. Bonaventure, *The Life of Our Lord and Saviour Jesus Christ* (New York: P. J. Kennedy & Sons, 1881).

more than the sterile rationalism and immanent frame of the modern world. They want to be enchanted; they deserve an enchanted Bible. Here's the thing: *A re-enchanted biblical text will depend on the re-enchantment of the people of God, for it takes an enchanted people to engage an enchanted text. It takes an enchanted people to evangelize and disciple people into an enchanted Christianity.*

It is tempting to believe that Christianity has gone too far down the road of secularization to have any chance of re-enchantment. I have hope, however, for a turn in things. We all feel a growing hunger for *more*: *more* real presence, *more* openness to transcendence, *more* participation in things divine, *more* embodiment, *more* of the imaginative, *more* of the Living Word. This book is my small offering toward that desire for *more*.

Re-enchanting God's people calls for a vision of humans as beings made in the image of a relational God and as those who, by the Holy Spirit, are capacitated to live in communion with God and others. Re-enchanting the people of God calls for an understanding of humans as a hypostatic union of spirit and flesh.

Made for Communion

The modern buffered self is an example of just how far we as humans have come from our primal identity. As those who are closed off, independent, and self-contained, we cannot fully know God, the world, and Scripture. It is a strange irony that we live in a time when humanity knows more than ever before, but our closed-off knowing of the world leaves us isolated and overwhelmed. Whereas knowledge was once power, it is now capable of bestowing a sense of powerlessness, especially in the age of the internet, in which we are confronted daily by an endless maze of possible knowledge.

Humans are not made to be mere "information receivers." We are created for the deep, relational, experiential knowing of *yada*. This form of knowing empowers us to experientially relate to God and the world. It allows us to see with the eyes of our heart. As creatures made in the image of God, we are created for love and fellowship with God and one another.

The doctrine of the Trinity is helpful in knowing how to talk about God. It is also important for discussions of what it means to be created in God's image. As the doctrine of the Trinity evolved during the first four centuries of the ancient church, major theologians attempted to explicate the nature of the *theologia*, God's mode of being (*ousia*) in relation to God's *oikonomia*, the communion of God with us through Christ in the Spirit. Now we ask: What is the nature of the triune life? How does that life interface with redeemed creation? Late in the fourth century, the Cappadocians were at the heart of efforts to answer this question. Out of these efforts came what is known as the Cappadocian formula: *mia ousia, treis hypostaseis* (one being, three persons). The doctrine of the Trinity is critical to our knowing God. As John Zizioulas writes, "The Holy Trinity is a *primordial* ontological concept and not a notion which is added to the divine substance or rather that follows it."[3]

The personhood of God has important implications for our relationship to God and to one another. To have an encounter with Jesus is to encounter the person of Jesus through the person of the Holy Spirit. God is not an abstract entity, inviting contemplation. Rather, God, existing as one being, three persons, invites us as persons into direct communion with the divine life. Andrew Root notes that the apostle Paul uses the phrase "in Christ" more than fifty times, while the phrases "in the Lord [Jesus/Jesus Christ]" and "in Christ Jesus our Lord" appear a total of forty times.[4] Root points out that, for Paul, these phrases reflect an ontological reality, one in which the human encounters (lives in) the transcendent. Root also discusses how difficult it is for those of us living in a secular age to wrap our minds around such a reality. How can the buffered selves living in the Age of Authenticity be open to such encounters? Such an idea of "being

3. John Zizioulas, *Being as Communion: Studies in Personhood and the Church* (Crestwood, NY: St. Vladimir's Seminary Press, 1997), 17.

4. Andrew Root, *Faith Formation in a Secular Age: Responding to the Church's Obsession with Youthfulness* (Grand Rapids: Baker Academic, 2017), 131.

in" counters the idea of the free-agent self. Indeed, it does, for as the apostle Paul would testify, "being in" Christ means dying to self: "I die every day" (1 Cor. 15:31); "To me, living is Christ and dying is gain" (Phil. 1:21); "I have been crucified with Christ" (Gal. 2:19).

From the perspective of the Cappadocians, hypostasis is a "kind of embodied personal spiritual reality that produces rich union without diminishment."[5] Herein lies the wonder: in our dying to self, we are not diminished but are fulfilled in our distinct personhood. Protestants have emphasized distinct personhood over against what we see as the Orthodox and Roman Catholic overemphasis on the "we" created in hypostatic union. Ziziolous, an Orthodox theologian, describes personhood as "beings in communion." For Ziziolous, the "we" of God's triune life flows into his understanding of the nature of human persons. Just as God's life is not one of closed individual selves, so the human "person is not a self-enclosed substantial entity, but rather an open relational entity," writes Miroslav Volf about Zizioulas's view. Furthermore, Volf says, "Just as God's life is ecstatic movement toward relationality, the person is ecstatic, designed for communion. As such, a person is essentially relational; it is itself only when it stands in a relation."[6]

Volf points out that Zizioulas understands God's trinitarian nature in a hierarchical pattern of relations in which "the relationship between the one (The Father) and the many (the Son and the Spirit) is asymmetrical in favor of the 'one.'"[7] This pattern of divine relations serves as the template for ecclesial relations. In critique of Zizioulas, Volf offers a vision of the triune life in which the "I" and the "we" are united in a creative tension. Made in the image of God, humans are a dialectical unity of the "I" and the "we." In other words, while we are made for relationship, we are also created as unique persons.

5. Root, *Faith Formation in a Secular Age*, 137–38.

6. Miroslav Volf, *After Our Likeness: The Church as the Image of the Trinity* (Grand Rapids: Eerdmans, 1998), 82.

7. Volf, *After Our Likeness*, 236.

In addition, we have the capacity to enter the fellowship of God's life, both corporately and individually.

In his 1953–54 Gifford lectures, John Macmurray challenged the modern "turn to the subject." His lectures are remarkable in their assessment of the problems arising from the self as reigning over an objective world. During the mid-twentieth century, most people were celebrating the human power to know and control the world. At this time, Macmurray warned of the isolation resulting from reducing the human to an "individual center of consciousness." He called for a view of the self as person: "Personal existence is constituted by relationship with other persons."[8] Macmurray identified the self as "agent." Even in relationship, the self maintains agency in embodied and operative interaction with the world. The self as agent does not objectify the world as an "it." Rather, the "'I' exists only in a 'You and I.'"[9]

It is important to see that, in relating to the Bible as Spirit-Word, persons enter this space as *relational beings with agency*, a powerful fusion of the "I" and the "we." The Holy Spirit works to blend these dynamics into a synergy, creating charismatic communities that offer what Volf describes as "an open ecclesial process."[10] "Relations between [persons expressing] charismata, modeled after the Trinity," writes Volf, "are reciprocal and symmetrical; all members of the church have charismata, and all are to engage their charismata for the good of all others."[11] In this model, both subjecthood and unity exist, with each having a participative, pneumatic quality.

The participative quality in open ecclesial communities allows for the Word to speak both corporately and personally. These communities are not a "free for all." Rather, ecclesial communities celebrate

8. John Macmurray, *The Self as Agent* (New York: Harper & Brothers, 1957), 11.

9. John Macmurray, *Persons in Relation* (New York: Harper & Brothers, 1961), 24. In his understanding of "I-You," Macmurray echoes Martin Buber's concept of "I-Thou." For Buber, the "I" is actualized through its participation in the other. As the supreme "Thou," God actualizes the true "I" of the human person. See Martin Buber, *I and Thou* (New York: Harper & Brothers, 1961).

10. Volf, *After Our Likeness*, 243.

11. Volf, *After Our Likeness*, 236.

the Spirit's filling of all flesh and endowing them with gifts in service to the church. Catherine Mowry LaCugna's vision of perichoresis is helpful here. She does not locate perichoresis exclusively within the intradivine sphere but sees this divine dance incorporating "the mystery of the one communion of all persons, divine as well as human." Through Christ, humanity is not absorbed into the divine dance. Rather, we are invited to participate as partners. "There are not two sets of communion—one among the divine persons, the other among human persons, with the latter supposed to replicate the former. The one perichoresis, the one mystery of communion includes God and humanity as beloved partners in the dance. This is what Jesus prayed for in the high-priestly prayer in John's Gospel (John 17:20–21)."[12] Created in the image of God, humans exist in a perichoretic pattern that is a dance of the personal and the corporate, the temporal and the eternal.[13]

The concept of personhood that is grounded in the triune life sees the true person as neither autonomous nor absorbed in others (heteronomy). True personhood has its life in theonomous identity, which comes from God and results in genuine communion with God and other persons. In this location, the integrity of the persons in communion is preserved. Jesus Christ is the full representation of a theonomous person. The Holy Spirit serves to facilitate the life of Christ in believers. "To be sure," observes LaCugna, "the Spirit does not change the human nature into a divine nature, but if substance is seen to derive from personhood, then the Spirit brings about an ontological union of God and the creature. . . . The Spirit deifies human beings, makes them holy, sets them free from sin, free from the conditions of the biological *hypostasis*, conforms them to the person of Christ."[14] Furthermore, just as the Spirit empowered and anointed the ministry of Jesus, so too does the Spirit serve to

12. Catherine Mowry LaCugna, *God for Us: The Trinity and the Christian Life* (New York: HarperCollins, 1973), 274.

13. See Cheryl Bridges Johns, "Transcripts of the Trinity: Reading the Bible in the Presence of God," *Ex Auditu* 30 (2014): 164.

14. LaCugna, *God for Us*, 297.

charismatically endow believers with ministry gifts, continuing the ministry of Jesus.

There is an understandable fear of an open ecclesial community becoming a community of chaos. However, as Volf notes, "Legal precautionary measures serve to create the space in which the complex mutual interdependence between individual charismatics and the congregation can be realized."[15] The New Testament provides examples of the apostle Paul's correction and instruction on the proper function of the charismata: "Let two or three prophets speak, and let the others weigh what is said, . . . for God is a God not of disorder but of peace" (1 Cor. 14:29, 33).

Scripture exists in service of the Spirit's work in the ontological union of God and the creature. It is able to facilitate the sanctification of human beings, making them holy and setting them free from sin. As noted in chapter 8, entering scriptural space is therefore both dangerous and wonderful. It is dangerous because, through the written Word, the Living Word bids us to take up our cross, follow him, and die to ourselves. It is wonderful because, by the power of the Spirit, we are given a taste of the life to come.

Scripture also serves to facilitate and define the parameters of the church's life. It invites us into the charismata and narrates the parameters of the exercise of spiritual gifts. There are not two separate spheres: one for the charismata and another for the Word. In the domain of Spirit-Word, the church, its elders, pastors, and teachers embody the joys of hypostatic union. I have a favorite childhood memory of people saying, as they left a church service, "Did we not sit together in heavenly places with Christ Jesus?"

Spirit-Flesh

As Spirit-Word, Scripture uniquely brings together the material with the divine. Humanity, likewise, is a unique synthesis of spirit and flesh. Persons do not exist as spirits who reside in flesh, waiting for the great

15. Volf, *After Our Likeness*, 243.

escape into the "real world." This dualism, inherited from the ancient Greeks, continues to plague Western Christianity. Rather, persons are a synergy of the material and the spiritual, prefiguring the resurrected life.

The Human Spirit

The human spirit is analogous to the divine Spirit. In 1 Corinthians, the apostle Paul attempts to tease out this unique relationship: "For the Spirit searches everything, even the depths of God. For what human being knows what is truly human except the human spirit that is within? So also no one comprehends what is truly God's except the Spirit of God" (2:10–11). Paul goes on to say that in order to participate in the deep mysteries and gifts found in the revelation of Christ, one must be in communion with the Spirit of God. When the human spirit joins with the divine Spirit, a person is able to enter the space that "no eye has seen, nor ear heard" (1 Cor. 2:9). In their creative book joining the field of quantum physics and Christian theology, James Loder and Jim Neidhardt suggest that modern culture offers two stark dualisms: (1) between the knowing subject and the known universe, and (2) between the created order and its Creator. The first dualism rejects any talk about the human spirit by which "creative acts of discovery as well as their appropriations occur"; the second "defeats for the modern mind any talk of the Holy Spirit by which the contingent bond between Creator and creation is continuously sustained." As long as these two dualisms prevail, we will continue to be what Søren Kierkegaard called "a spiritless generation," according to Loder and Neidhardt.[16] As an alternative to the dualisms, they offer as an alternative a "Chalcedonian-like union of the Divine Spirit with the

16. James E. Loder and W. Jim Neidhardt, *The Knight's Move: The Relational Logic of the Spirit in Theology and Science* (Colorado Springs: Helmers & Howard, 1992), 31. For Loder and Neidhardt, Einstein's theory of relativity did not make everything relative. They reference Einstein—"God is deep but not devious"—in support of their belief that the depths of quantum physics, the deep mysteries of the ordered and created universe, are to be known spirit to Spirit.

human spirit, giving evidence that the human is heir of the renewal by God of all creation" (Rom. 8:16).[17]

In the relationship between the divine Spirit and the human spirit, we cannot simply dissolve the human spirit into the divine. The two are distinct, but they are not mutually exclusive. The image of God as human spirit calls out to the divine. Being filled with the Holy Spirit is not absorption; rather, it fulfills the promise that the human spirit can exist in relational harmony and delight with the divine Spirit. Indeed, the Holy Spirit bears witness with our spirits that we are the children of God, and we cry, "Abba! Father!" (Rom. 8:15).

As spirit, the human person carries the power of *ecstasy* (Greek: *ekstasis*) as a way to self-transcendence. This capacity is part of being made in the image of God, for God's life is ecstatic, continually reaching outward in love, spilling out his "glorification in the economy," as LaCugna writes. She continues: "Praise is the mode of return, 'matching' God's movement of exodus. God creates out of glory, for glory. . . . Both God and the human person go outside of themselves so that each may become united in the other."[18] In this union, the mystery of the other is not diminished, nor is the other's mystery ever totally expressed or grasped.

Ecstasy has both mystical and sexual dynamics. Both the human yearning for God and sexual desire between two persons are expressions of intense desire. Mystical readings of books such as the Song of Songs bring the two forms together. On one level, Song of Songs expresses human ecstasy; on another level (mystical), it expresses the ecstatic joining between God and humanity.

As ecstatic, the human spirit is open, especially to "a God who exceeds our horizon of expectation and comes unexpectedly," as James K. A. Smith says. The unexpected advent of the incarnation, the unexpected coming of the Spirit at Pentecost, and God's Spirit working among the gentiles are examples of the ecstatic God breaking into the lives of those with an open spirit. Having an open spirit does not

17. Loder and Niedhardt, *Knight's Move*, 33.
18. LaCugna, *God for Us*, 350–51.

mean "kissing one's brain good-bye." Rather, it means being open to having one's ideas and expectations of God changed by God himself.[19]

When believers enter the sacred space of Scripture with a spirit of openness, deep calls to deep, and through engagement with the text, the human spirit reaches out to join with the divine. Spirit-Word joins with spirit-flesh. The Bible serves as a portal for this mystical union. As Spirit-Word, it opens the door, allowing the light from the future to stream into the present. In this light, deep calls to deep, and the ecstasy of God embraces the ecstasy of the human spirit. We are home.

The joining of Spirit-Word with spirit-flesh does not discount use of reason. It is, however, transrational, operating beyond the limitations of purely cognitive reason in truly seeing and knowing the world. The best forms of study are those that can be employed without losing the dynamics of the transrational. I prefer the inductive approach to Bible study. Its focus on the literary and relational nature of the text facilitates the imaginative Spirit's role in helping us see the connections, literary patterns, beautiful chiastic structures, and deep relational dynamics found in the biblical text. Inductive Bible study's call for epistemic humility and a spirit of openness asks that we stay open to the decentering power of otherness found in the text.

The ecstasy of the human spirit flows out of the affections. The affections are the core of one's being, uniting reason and passion. Writes Steven Land, "Affections are abiding dispositions which dispose the person toward God and the neighbor in ways appropriate to their source and goal in God."[20] Feelings come and go, but the affections are constant. In the affective form of knowing, the eyes of the heart are employed, allowing the human spirit to relate to the divine.

The central Christian affection is love. John Wesley understood love as the core human affection, and perfect love as wholehearted devotion to God. Wesley exhorts his listeners to "be most zealous of

19. James K. A. Smith, *Thinking in Tongues: Pentecostal Contributions to Christian Philosophy* (Grand Rapids: Eerdmans, 2010), 34.

20. Steven J. Land, *Pentecostal Spirituality: A Passion for the Kingdom* (Sheffield: Sheffield Academic, 2001), 136.

all for love, the queen of all graces, the highest perfection in heaven or earth, the very image of the invisible God."[21]

Smith offers "a nonreductionistic understanding of human persons as embodied agents of love." He notes that "this Augustinian model of personhood resists the rationalism and quasi-rationalism of the earlier models by shifting the center of gravity of human identity . . . down from the heady regions of mind closer to the central regions of our bodies, in particular, our *kardia*—our gut or heart." Smith believes humans "inhabit the world . . . not primarily as thinkers . . . but as more affective, embodied creatures."[22] Smith helps us understand that the person is first and foremost a desiring creature. Love or desire is not extraneous to being human: it is a basic structural feature.

If we envision human beings as embodied, desiring creatures, then it is easy to see how modern approaches to the Bible fail to engage us. They leave us standing by the wayside on our way home to God. These approaches are like reading a map and assuming that, in reading the map, we have taken the trip to where we need to go. George Barna's "Christian worldview" reading of the Bible offers the promise of "thinking like Jesus."[23] But in order to live like Jesus, we must have a deeper understanding of our relationship with the Bible, one that encourages us to "love like Jesus." In Smith's view, "The affective and emotional core of identity . . . needs to be reformed and redirected. Changes in a *way of life* will not take place until that affective core is reached."[24]

The Embodied Human

Embodiment is one of the key features of re-enchantment. Re-enchanting the natural world involves reuniting the material and spiritual dimensions of the cosmos. Re-enchanting Christianity involves

21. John Wesley, "Sermon XCVII: On Zeal," in vol. 7 of *The Works of the Rev. John Wesley in Ten Volumes* (New York: J. & J. Harper, 1826), 67.

22. James K. A. Smith, *Desiring the Kingdom: Worship, Worldview, and Cultural Formation* (Grand Rapids: Baker Academic, 2009), 47.

23. See George Barna, *Think Like Jesus: Make the Right Decision Every Time* (Brentwood, TN: Integrity, 2003).

24. Smith, *Thinking in Tongues*, 77.

sacramentally embodying grace within the life of the church. Re-enchanting the Bible involves bringing the Bible's material existence into the life of God's economy. Re-enchanting the people of God calls for bringing spirit and flesh together into a dynamic holism.

The Moravian philosopher Edmund Husserl believed that the lived body (and not the mind) is central to experience. The body plays a key role in making sense of the world. Husserl established the school of philosophy known as phenomenology, a field of study that investigates how people actually experience the world. Building on Husserl, French philosopher Maurice Merleau-Ponty turned the Cartesian notion "I think, therefore I am" into "The world is not what I think, but what I live."[25] Human beings do not just have bodies: we are bodies. We live in the world in and through our bodies. Our communities, families, and churches are rich ecologies of embodied people.

Smith writes, "An affirmation of embodiment is essential to the incarnational principle at the heart of Christian confession. The story that God tells us about who we are begins with God's making us flesh, quickening the flesh of Adam *as* a material, embodied creature—and *then* saying it was 'very good.'"[26] The affirmation of embodiment is expressed in the birth of Jesus, his death, and his resurrection. The embodied, risen Jesus as firstborn of the new creation gives us a hope for our own embodiment in the consummation of that creation.

The image of people as "thinking things," whose worship is primarily cognitive, is a recent invention. Smith points out that it came about primarily as a result of a secularization fostering the idea that "significance no longer inheres in things; rather, meaning and significance are a property of minds who perceive meaning internally."[27] In this world, the body does not possess inherent meaning. Like all other parts of the natural world, it suffers the fate of excarnation—the

25. Maurice Merleau-Ponty, *Phenomenology of Perception*, trans. Donald Landes (New York: Routledge, 2013), lxxx.

26. Smith, *Thinking in Tongues*, 60.

27. James K. A. Smith, *How (Not) to Be Secular: Reading Charles Taylor* (Grand Rapids: Eerdmans, 2014), 86. Also see Charles Taylor, *A Secular Age* (Cambridge, MA: Harvard University Press, 2007), 29.

evacuation of the sacred from the material. In the modern version of the Christian life, the mind leads people into belief, into what Barna describes as *thinking* like Jesus. The body tags along as an interloper.

Before our secular, disenchanted age, Christian worship was embodied: people taken down into rivers of baptism and raised to life again, hands raised in praise, laying on of hands during prayer, anointing with oil, ashen crosses placed on foreheads, the sign of the cross on the chest, walking pilgrimages, kneeling or falling prostrate in prayer, and dancing in the Spirit. This incarnational form of worship continues in the majority world. It can be seen in varying forms within Pentecostal and liturgical churches.

Smith gives a poignant description of his initiation into embodied worship after growing up in a "rabidly fundamentalist and cessationist tradition":

> I remember how *physically* difficult it was to get my body to participate in worship. I remember the utter awkwardness of raising a hand in praise, almost as if it were cemented to my side. But then I also remember the remarkable sense of release—the almost sacramental dispensation of grace and liberation and renewal that seemed to flow down through up-stretched arms, as if the very positioning of my body opened channels for grace to flow where it couldn't otherwise. I remember the remarkable charge of grace that would come with a hand laid on my shoulder in prayer—the very embodied, material connection that was solidified by touch.[28]

A sacramental vision of the Bible, one in which the material dimension of the text serves as a sanctified means of grace, calls for a sacramental, embodied vision of the human person. A sacramental vision of the human understands the body as making grace visible and serving as a channel in receiving and extending that grace.

Pope John Paul II had a particular interest in developing a theology of the body, so much so that between 1979 and 1984 he delivered a series of 129 talks on the topic. In one of the talks, he says, "The body,

28. Smith, *Thinking in Tongues*, 61.

and in fact, only the body is capable of making visible the invisible: the spiritual and the divine."[29] Timothy Tennent echoes the sentiment of John Paul II: "A theology of the body means that we understand the body as not merely a biological category but supremely as a theological category, designed for God's revelatory and saving purposes. In short, the body makes the invisible mysteries of God's nature and redemption manifest and visible as a tangible marker in the world."[30]

The body, in making visible the invisible mysteries of God's nature and redemption, serves as a means of revelation. Before Scripture was written, it was spoken. The word came through Moses and the prophets, through the spoken words of embodied Jesus, and through the teachings of the apostles. The written Word and the spoken or Living Word are not two Words. Rather, they are two forms of the same Word of God.

Scripture continues to serve as the primary means of God's revelation without consuming all revelation into itself (closed canon and ongoing revelation). Human bodies also serve to continue the revelation of God's economy. The mysterious unity in marriage of two embodied people—male and female—shows forth God's revelation of covenant love. The birth of a baby is a revelatory event of Emmanuel, God with us. Human creative action, when brought into harmony with God's creative intentions, furthers revelation. The mysterious embodiment of the church, within whom the Spirit grants gifts, continues the revelation of God's intention to restore all things.

As embodied, sacramental beings, humans are made not only to enter the sacred space of Scripture; we are also made to bodily inhabit the revelatory book of nature. It is impossible to read the Bible and not catch a glimpse of a time when people were more deeply embodied in the natural world than we are today. A few years ago, I did a study on the verdant life expressed in the Song of Songs. I was taken aback by its depiction of a rich and fertile world. Not only are the

29. John Paul II, "The Redemption of the Body and the Sacramentality of Marriage (Theology of the Body)," 19:4. For the full pdf version, see https://d2y1pz2y630308.cloudfront.net/2232/documents/2016/9/theology_of_the_body.pdf.

30. Timothy C. Tennent, *For the Body: Recovering a Theology of Gender, Sexuality, and the Human Body* (Nashville: Zondervan Reflective, 2020), 14.

characters filled with desire for each other; they also take pleasure in the vibrant ecology of their environment.

Enchanted people often describe the world as singing to them and they to it. Restoration ecologist Suprabha Seshan, who works in the jungles of the southern Indian mountains, sees herself living in harmony with the living world around her. She sings to all the creatures living in the mountains, she says, "partly because they sing so sweetly to me all the time!"[31] Through her singing, Seshan weaves herself into the world.

In modernity's turn to the subject and the resulting objectification of the world, nature lost its integrity and its inherent right to live. It became an object to be acted on, a depository of "natural resources," and, in some cases, something to be conquered. Mountaintop removal, the process of blasting off the tops of mountains to more quickly and cheaply harvest coal, has left a trail of wrecked ecology. Due to the polluting runoff, communities living near these mountains have lost access to clean water. The natural habitat of trees, plants, and animals has been disrupted. This scene bears witness to the power of disenchantment to create wastelands.

In his foreword to the English edition of Peter Wohlleben's *The Hidden Life of Trees*, Tim Flannery writes, "We read in fairy tales of trees with human faces, trees that can talk, and sometimes walk."[32] That's all for children, and we all know that fairy tales are not real, right? Perhaps we should think again. Wohlleben, a forest manager who works in the Eifel mountains of Germany, vividly describes the ecosystem of forests as having their own forms of friendship, language, love, and social security. Hidden beneath trees lies a complex communication system, one that sends out nutrients to weaker trees. Leaves send out electrical signals when attacked by invading insects; in response to these signals, defensive compounds mount an attack on the invaders. Mother trees nourish the young, keeping them in shade

31. Quoted in Sharon Blackie, *The Enchanted Life: Unlocking the Magic of the Everyday* (Toronto: House of Anansi, 2018), 119.

32. Tim Flannery, foreword to Peter Wohlleben, *The Hidden Life of Trees: What They Feel, How They Communicate—Discoveries from a Secret World*, trans. Jane Billinghurst (London: William Collins, 2016), vii.

so that their growth is slow enough to create strong trunks and limbs. Trees are open systems living in harmony with many thousands of types of fungi that reside in the connective root system beneath the soil. Wohlleben describes their interactions: "First, the fungi listen in on what the tree has to say through its underground structures. Depending on whether that information is useful for them, the fungi begin to produce plant hormones that direct the tree's cell growth to their advantage." In return for their services, the fungi "demand up to a third of the tree's total food production."[33]

The more we learn about the complex, integrative life of the world around us, the more enchanted we become. Who cannot help but be awestruck when looking out at the massive breadth of the cosmos? Who cannot but stand in wonder at the world's oldest tree, a ninety-five-hundred-year-old spruce in Sweden? Who does not wonder about the intricate and beautiful communication between massive whales? Attending to the harmony of creation puts us in harmony with God.

As spirit-flesh, we are made to have a deep connection to the natural world. The creation, as suspended and held within God, invites us to join with it in holy praise to and in communion with the Creator. How do we do this?

The practice of mindfulness is a popular means of helping people release their anxiety and overcome distractions. It can take many forms but typically involves times of meditation in which people are fully present and aware of where they are. To practice mindfulness is "to fully attend." Studies show that mindfulness involves the prefrontal cortex and parietal lobes, sections of the brain linked to attention control. Mindfulness asks people to pay attention to their bodies, but in the practice, the priority is *mental focus*.

To find enchantment, the body needs to look upon the natural world. The practice of what Sharon Blackie calls "bodyfulness" carries us deeper into connection with the natural world than does mindfulness. Blackie describes bodyfulness as a shift "from feeling that your body is an object you control with your mind, to realising that mind,

33. Wohlleben, *Hidden Life of Trees*, 51.

or intelligence, is located throughout your body."[34] The emphasis in knowing is not on the prefrontal cortex but is distributed throughout the body.

In the 1990s, people in Japan began studying how time spent in forests decreased blood pressure, elevated mood, and contributed to overall wellness. The Japanese minister of agriculture, forest, and fisheries coined the term *shinrin-yoku*, which is loosely translated as "forest bathing." Forest bathing involves spending time in nature, especially forests. This time is unlike a fast hike in which someone might try to see how many miles they can trek in one day. Rather, it involves slow "forest time"—exploring, breathing deeply, and meditating on the sights and sounds of nature. The key to forest bathing is "bodyfulness," becoming porous selves, allowing our bodies as well as our spirits to absorb the ecology around us. Such experience both centers us in the earth and expands us beyond ourselves.

We are called to have an enchanted relationship with the two books, nature and Scripture, so it should come as no surprise that there is a correlation between our lack of connection to the natural world and a disenchanted view of the Bible. When one objectifies the world, lording over it as supreme subject, using its verdant life as a "bag of resources" without regard for the ecological dynamics, the damaged ecological imaginary that results can easily be transferred into other realms. It leads us to objectify people, using them as tools in our own mastery of the world. It leads us to objectify the Bible, reducing it to the status of a tool in our perceived spiritual "takeover" of the world. The Bible's beautiful ecology, its bountiful life, and its status as a sanctified vessel of revelation give way to the reigning human subject. Nothing good can come from this ontological move.

Putting It All Together

Created in the image of God, human persons are made to live in an enchanted world. We are designed for *more* than our current state

34. Blackie, *Enchanted Life*, 108.

of being. We are beautifully designed for *more* of the real presence of God in our lives, for living in deep communion with God and in relational harmony with one another. We are made for *more* awareness of the human spirit and its capacity for union with the divine Spirit, as well as its capacity for its own self-transcendence. We are designed to be hopeful, open persons, living in expectation of the ecstatic God breaking into our lives. We are lovers, people whose affections are guided by the eyes of our hearts.

We are embodied creatures whose flesh the Creator deems "good." Our bodies sacramentally house and convey grace. The Creator calls us to bodily embrace the natural world as a fellow creation deemed "good." We have the capacity to join with the groaning of all creation as we wait for the renewal of all things.

All these capacities make us fit for an enchanted Bible, one in which Spirit-Word joins with spirit-flesh as we come to know and love God. We are designed to dwell in the mysterious ethos of the Bible. In this space we find the gift of the triune life, the power of revelation, and the harmony of Spirit-Word. We are uniquely able to enter the enchanting dimensions of Holy Scripture. Here the *mystērion* waits to be discovered, and the space between the supernatural and natural grows very thin. Through the power of the pneumatic imagination, we are invited to sit together in heavenly places with Christ Jesus. We are uniquely designed to heed the call of abjection that echoes throughout the chambers of Scripture, where taking up our Bibles means taking up the cross.

Index